Blue Ribbon book of herb and spice cookery

D1100323

Contents

© 1971 Brooke Bond Oxo Ltd., Leon House, High Street, Croydon, England.

Prepared for the Blue Ribbon Herb and Spice Kitchen by
Kingsway Public Relations Ltd., 83 Kingsway, London, WC 2B 6SH, England.

Designed and produced by The Hamlyn Publishing Group Ltd.,
42 The Centre, Feltham, Middlesex, England.

Printed in Holland by Smeets, Weert

ISBN 0 600 31265 8

Introduction

Blue Ribbon herbs, spices and seasonings are carefully selected from various countries in the world to ensure that only the highest quality is used.

The term 'spice' is sometimes used to include herbs, spices, aromatic seeds and the innumerable blends and seasonings available to flavour food. Herbs are the leaves of plants which grow in temperate climates; spices are the parts of plants which usually grow in the tropics; aromatic seeds are the seeds or fruits of plants which grow in tropical or temperate climates. Also included under the heading of 'spices' are dehydrated vegetables such as garlic and onion which are then powdered, flaked or minced. Seasonings are obtained by blending herbs and spices; sometimes other flavourings are also added.

We hope you will have fun trying the recipes in this book and experimenting with new ones using Blue Ribbon herbs, spices and seasonings.

Note
At the time of going to press all varieties of 'spices' listed in this book were available. However, it may be necessary to withdraw one or two 'spices' at a later date.

Historical background to Herbs & Spices

Archaeologists believe that the knowledge of seasoning food goes back at least 50,000 years. Primitive man depended on wild animals and plants for his food and well-being and it would appear that he was soon able to learn which were good to eat, which had healing properties and to recognise the poisonous ones. Man's search for good herbs and spices (dried fruits, roots and berries) gradually became more purposeful. Besides their uses in seasoning and preserving food, succeeding civilisations came to realise their medicinal properties, endowed them with magical properties and used them in religious rituals and ceremonies. Herbs, spices and their oils became essential too for toilet preparations.

Herbs were probably first used in the areas where they were indigenous—the Mediterranean regions and southern Asia. Sometimes they were transported as dried herbs, carried by travellers and conquering armies—the Romans are thought to have brought about 400 different plants to Britain. When the Europeans colonised America, Africa and other parts of the

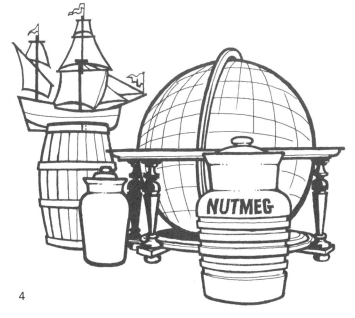

world they too introduced the herbs they valued most to their new countries.

The Babylonians and Assyrians cultivated herbs in gardens. Among the herbs listed for the use of Assyrian doctors and chemists were oregano and thyme. Mint is recorded as being used in an Assyrian ritual to appease the Fire-god. The Egyptians too made extensive use of herbs. In one of the earliest, simplest embalming processes, sweet marjoram has been identified. A herb mentioned in Exodus 30-23 as being used by the ancient Hebrews is sweet calamus, commonly known as sweet flag.

The medicine of the ancient world depended largely on the knowledge of herbalists and the medical school of Alexandria was renowned in this field. Greek writers made valuable contributions to ancient botanical and medical science; the most renowned treatise is reputed to have been written by Hippocrates in the 4th century B.C.

The Romans grew and used many varieties of herbs but with the decline of the Roman Empire, herbs were gradually forgotten. Centuries later, in the early Middle ages, herbs were re-introduced by monks and were once again extensively used. Their popularity declined when, as a result of the Industrial Revolution, synthetic flavourings for foods dominated the market. In recent years the demand for herbs has revived, encouraged by the development of new techniques of drying which help retain their flavour and colour.

Aromatic seeds are classed as spices and almost all are indigenous to the Mediterranean regions and Asia. Like herbs, these dried seeds were first used in the areas in which they grew, and were similarly transported by travellers, soldiers and colonists. They now flourish in many temperate and tropical regions of the world.

Spices are indigenous to tropical Eastern countries and could not be grown locally. They thus assumed considerable commercial value and the trade in spices has a long, exciting and violent history.

The spice trade probably began in Mesopotamia, the cradle of civilisation, with the exchange of herbs and aromatic seeds between communities. As people travelled further afield, the dried aromatics of one part of the East would find their way to another and at some indeterminate time, caravan routes were established. Originating in India, Ceylon, China or Java these caravans travelled through the Middle East to the Eastern Mediterranean and later to Europe, for at least 5,000 years. The classic route followed was to cross the Indus at Attock, travel through Peshawar and across the eastern Himalayas by the Khyber Pass; from there it went through Afghanistan and Persia (Iran) south to Babylon. This route was later extended west to the eastern Mediterranean and Europe. When the spices reached the Mediterranean, the trade was controlled by groups of merchants in towns such as Alexandria. Spice merchants became wealthy and powerful.

The Phoenicians controlled the trade at one time; they established trading stations and also provided ships. The Arabs later gained the monopoly which they had for centuries until the Portuguese discovered the sea route to the East. Buyers of spices were often ignorant of their origin, supposing them to come from Arabia; the crafty Arabian traders encouraged this belief, inventing fantastic tales to keep the curious ignorant.

There was a decline in the spice trade following the fall of the Roman Empire in the 5th century A.D., until the crusades. In exchange for their help to the crusaders, the Italians received trading privileges in the conquered lands and the Venetian merchants soon became all powerful. At the time of the last crusade, a young Venetian, Marco Polo set out on a journey which lasted 24 years and he reached China in 1275. He became a favourite of the Kubla Khan, travelling extensively round Asia where he actually saw spices growing.

During the Middle Ages, spices were distributed by merchants in the mediaeval town markets throughout Europe. Later, a more orderly marketing of goods developed, and the spice merchants formed their own guilds. In England in the 12th century the Pepperers Guild was formed by the Spicers of Sopers Lane; this became the Worshipful Company of Grocers in 1345. Peppercorns were so valuable that London dockers had to wear suits without pockets to prevent stealing; only the rich could afford to buy these valuable eastern spices. To prevent the adulteration of spices the first pure food law in history was passed in England in 1447.

The Renaissance of learning in Europe spurred other nations to attempt to break the monopoly of the spice trade by the

Venetians. The search began for a sea route to the East. In Portugal, Prince Henry the Navigator encouraged Portuguese sailors to attempt to find this route. In 1487, Bartholomew Diaz rounded the Cape of Good Hope and in 1498, Vasco da Gama eventually reached India. These achievements threatened not only the Venetian spice merchants but the merchants of the Middle East as well.

Meanwhile, in 1492, Christopher Columbus, sailing west in his search for India, discovered America. He sailed under the Spanish flag and it was the Spaniards who introduced new spices into Europe — allspice and the capsicum spices (paprika, chillies and sweet peppers). The Spaniards thought the allspice berries were peppercorns and allspice is still sometimes known as Jamaica pepper. This spice was used to preserve smoked meat which was known as 'boucan' and the pirates' dependence on this earned them the name of 'boucaneers' which became buccaneers.

By this time the Portuguese had the monopoly of the spice trade and the Spanish, English and Dutch intensified their efforts to find the sea route. Ferdinand Magellan, a Portuguese sailor, sailed in Spanish ships and reached the East by sailing west in 1521. Sir Francis Drake undertook a similar voyage, reaching the Spice Islands in 1579. However it was the Dutch who succeeded in breaking the power of the Portuguese. Cornelis van Houtman reached the Spice Islands in 1596 and by the middle of the 17th century the Dutch controlled the cinnamon trade in Ceylon. Some years later they owned the ports on the Malabar coast, then moved to Java. East India trading companies were formed, first by a group of English merchants in 1600, then the Dutch and much later the French.

Towards the end of the 18th century, the Dutch eventually began to lose their monopoly of the spice trade when plants were smuggled out of the Spice Islands to be introduced into French and English territories beyond their control. Spices then began to be grown in other tropical regions and were more readily available. No other nation ever regained the monopoly of the world spice trade. Although no longer such a priceless commodity, spices are still highly valued in the twentieth century. Modern communications allow easy, fast access to all parts of the world and this enables Blue Ribbon to obtain top quality herbs and spices wherever they are grown.

Location & uses of Herbs & Spices

Blue Ribbon herbs and spices are selected from the countries which produce the best quality. In the following list, the country from which Blue Ribbon usually obtain the herb or spice is mentioned after the herb or spice name. The map reference number (i.e. Basil M6) indicates the country supplying the particular herb or spice to Blue Ribbon. The general uses of each herb and spice are indicated as a guide (for map see pages 16—17).

Herbs

Basil/France   M 6

Also known as sweet basil. The dried leaves of a plant belonging to the Mint family. Native to India and Iran; cultivated in Europe, Asia and the U.S.A.

Uses Soups, stews, egg, tomato and vegetable dishes.

Bay Leaves/Turkey   O 7

The dried leaves of an evergreen tree belonging to the Laurel family. Native to, and cultivated in, Mediterranean countries. The leaves have a bitter, aromatic taste and an agreeable odour.

Sold as whole and ground bay leaves.

Uses Used widely in meat, game, poultry, fish and vegetable dishes, soups and stews.
Ground bay leaves also used in pickling.

Chervil/Holland   N 6

The dried leaves of a plant belonging to the Carrot family. Native to the Black Sea and Caspian Sea regions; also cultivated in Europe and the U.S.A. Has a delicate anise flavour.

Uses Soups, salad dressings, sauces, fish, meat, egg and cheese dishes, vegetables.

Chives/U.S.A.   D 7

The accelerated freeze dried leaves of a plant belonging to the Lily family. Known in China in 3,000 B.C., arrived in Europe in the 16th century. Cultivated widely. Onion flavour, but milder.

Uses Add to liquids — sauces, salad dressings, soups, casseroles; cream cheese and egg dishes.

Marjoram/Cyprus   O 8

The dried leaves, with or without flowering tops, of a plant belonging to the Mint family. Native to the Mediterranean region and western Asia; cultivated in most European countries and Asia. Fragrant aroma and slightly bitterish taste.

Sold as ground marjoram.

Uses Soups, stews (especially lamb or mutton), fish, egg and poultry dishes, vegetables, salads and stuffings.

Mint/Morocco   M 8

The dried leaves and flowering tops of plants belonging to the Mint family. Of the several species cultivated, peppermint and spearmint are used in the spice trade. Both are native to Europe and Asia; cultivated as well in North and South America and North Africa. Sweetish, strong aroma and pungent taste.

Uses Soups, stews, potato dishes, sauces, salads, drinks and confections.

Oregano/Portugal   M 7

The dried leaves and flowering tops of a plant belonging to the Mint family. Native to the Mediterranean region and western Asia; cultivated in Europe, Asia and Mexico. Strong odour, bitter taste.

Sold as whole and ground oregano.

Uses Soups, meat, fish, egg, cheese and vegetable dishes, sauces, pizza and tomato dishes.

Parsley/England   **M 6**

The dried leaves of a plant belonging to the Carrot family. Believed to be a native of Sardinia; extensively cultivated in Europe and North America. Must be dried rapidly to avoid the loss of the oil, which gives it is characteristic flavour, and to ensure a good, green colour.

Uses Numerous uses in soups, meat, fish, poultry and egg dishes, sauces, salad dressings and vegetables.

Rosemary/Portugal   **M 7**

The dried leaves of a shrub belonging to the Mint family. Native to the Mediterranean region; cultivated over most of Europe and in the U.S.A. Bitterish taste.

Uses Meat (especially lamb), poultry, fish and egg dishes, soups, sauces, vegetables and salads.

Sage/Italy   **N 7**

The dried leaves of a shrub belonging to the Mint family. Native to the Mediterranean region; cultivated in southern European countries and North America.

Sold as rubbed and ground sage.

Uses Pork, duck and other meats, in stuffings for meat or fish, in melted butter to serve with onions and marrow.

Savory/Yugoslavia   **O 7**

Also known as summer savory. The dried leaves and flowering tops of a plant belonging to the Mint family. Native to southern Europe; cultivated in most parts of Europe and North America.

Sold as ground savory.

Uses Soups, meat, poultry and egg dishes, sauces and salads.

Tarragon/Yugoslavia   **O 7**

The dried leaves of a plant belonging to the Sunflower family. Believed to be a native of Siberia; cultivated in Europe and North America. There are two varieties – Russian and French. Taste is reminiscent of anise.

Uses Gives a delicate flavour to meat, chicken, egg and tomato dishes. Also used in soups and sauces such as tartare.

Thyme/France   **M 6**

The dried leaves and flowering tops of a plant belonging to the Mint family. Native to the Mediterranean region and southern Europe; cultivated extensively in Europe, North Africa and North America. An aromatic plant with a pungent taste.

Uses In bouquet garni. Also for meat, poultry and fish dishes, soups, sauces and stuffings.

Spices and Aromatic Seeds

Allspice/Jamaica   **H 9**

Also known as Jamaica pepper. The dried fruit of an evergreen tree belonging to the Myrtle family. Native to the West Indies; also cultivated in Central America. Called 'Allspice' because its flavour resembles a combination of cinnamon, nutmeg and cloves. Has a fragrant aroma reminiscent of cloves.

Sold as whole and ground allspice.

Uses Both forms can be used to flavour meat and vegetable dishes, pickles and preserves.
Whole used as well in soups and fish dishes.
Ground used as well in mincemeat, puddings, cakes and drinks.

Anise Seed/Spain   **M 7**

The dried fruit of a plant belonging to the Carrot family. Native to Egypt; cultivated in both hot and temperate climates. The fruit is tiny, brown and oval with a liquorice flavour.

Uses Fruit pies, bread, cakes, biscuits and other confections.

Caraway Seed/Holland   N 6

The separate carpels of the dried fruit of a plant belonging to
the Carrot family. Native to Europe and western Asia; cultivated
in many parts of the world. Holland produces the best quality.
Flavour similar to, though stronger than, anise seed.

Uses Confections, bread, biscuits, cakes, cheese, soups,
sauces and poultry dishes.

Cardamom/India   S10

The dried fruit of a plant belonging to the Ginger family. Native
to India; cultivated as well in Ceylon and Central America. The
fruit consists of a three-celled capsule, each cell containing
a number of seeds. The fruits are harvested carefully by hand
before they are fully mature; they are then cured and dried and
carefully sorted by hand. The whole cardamom has an aromatic
aroma.

Sold as ground cardamom.

Uses In curry powder, meat dishes, cakes and pastries.

Cayenne/East Africa and China   P 11; V 8

Made from dried ripe fruits, 2 – 3 inches long, of a species of
capsicum, a plant belonging to the Potato family. Native to
tropical America; cultivated in many tropical, sub-tropical and
temperate regions. Ground mechanically then sifted through a
fine screen to produce the pepper.

Uses To give a hot flavour to sauces, fish, vegetable, egg and
cheese dishes.

Celery Seed/India   S 10

The dried fruit of a plant belonging to the Carrot family. Native
to southern Europe and Northern Africa; cultivated in Europe,
India, Japan and the U.S.A. Has a fresh celery aroma and taste.

Used in Blue Ribbon celery salt (see page 21).

Uses Soups, sauces, salads, salad dressings, pickles and egg
dishes.

Chillies/Zanzibar   **P 11**

There are numerous varieties: all are very pungent capsicum fruits of plants belonging to the Potato family. Native to tropical America; cultivated in many tropical, sub-tropical and temperate regions. Chillies are fiery, should not be tasted and should be handled with extreme care.

Uses Use sparingly in sea food, meat, pasta, egg, tomato and Mexican dishes, pickles.

Cinnamon/China   **V 8/9; U 9**

There are two types, Ceylon cinnamon and cassia cinnamon. Both are made from the dried bark of evergreen trees belonging to the Laurel family. Ceylon cinnamon is produced chiefly in Ceylon, cassia cinnamon in China, Cambodia, Vietnam and Indonesia.

Sold as ground cassia cinnamon. Cinnamon is also available in sticks.

Uses Bread, cakes, biscuits, pies, milk puddings, hot drinks. Also used with fruit and pickling spice.

Cloves/Zanzibar and Madagascar   **P 11; Q 12**

The dried unopened flower buds of an evergreen tree belonging to the Myrtle family. Native to the Moluccas (Spice Islands); cultivated as well in Madagascar, Zanzibar, India, Ceylon and other hot climates. Cloves need careful handling when drying to preserve the flavour and prevent the heads from breaking. The odour and taste are pronounced.

Sold as whole and ground cloves.

Uses Meat dishes, spiced fruit puddings and hot drinks and in pickling meat and fruit.

Coriander Seed/Rumania and Bulgaria   **O 7**

The dried fruit of a plant belonging to the Carrot family. Known to ancient civilisations; native to the Mediterranean and Near East regions; cultivated as well in India, Mexico, Argentina, the U.S.A. and England.

Uses Soups, poultry, sausages, stuffing, salads, cakes, biscuits, pastries and in mixed pickles.

Cumin Seed/Iran   **Q 8**

The dried fruit of a plant belonging to the Carrot family. Native to Egypt and the Mediterranean region; cultivated as well in Argentina, India, China and Iran.

Sold as ground cumin seed.

Uses Cheese, rice, meat, fish and egg dishes, bread, curries, stuffed eggs, soups.

Dill Seed/China   **V 8/9; U 9**

The dried fruit, consisting of united or separate carpels, of a plant belonging to the Carrot family. Native to Mediterranean countries and southern Russia; cultivated in Europe, India, China and North America. Flavour faintly reminiscent of caraway.

Uses Soups, sauces, cheese spreads, salads, pickles and fish, meat, vegetable and egg dishes.

Fennel Seed/China and India   **V 8; S 10**

The dried fruit of a plant belonging to the Carrot family. Native to southern Europe and Asia Minor; use spread by the conquering Romans; cultivated in Europe, North Africa, Asia Minor, India, Japan, China, Argentina and the U.S.A. Taste suggestive of anise.

Uses Soups, sauces, salads, fish and meat dishes, pickles, bread, pastries and confections.

Fenugreek/Morocco   **M 8**

The yellowish-brown, flat, hard seeds of a plant belonging to the Pea family. Native to southern Europe; cultivated in France, Lebanon, Morocco, India, Argentina. Aroma is reminiscent of burnt sugar, taste is mealy.

Used in Blue Ribbon salad seasoning (see page 24).

Uses Chutneys and in curry powder.

Herb and Spice Map

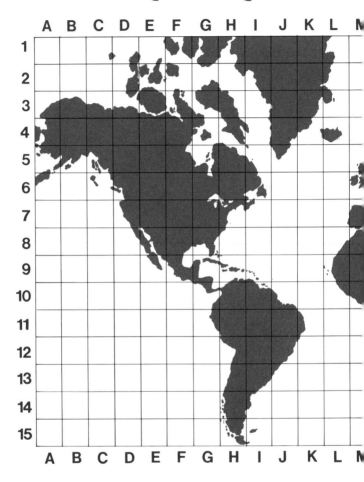

The map references for the countries from which Blue Ribbon usually obtain their supplies are given in the list of herbs and spices (pages 8 – 23).

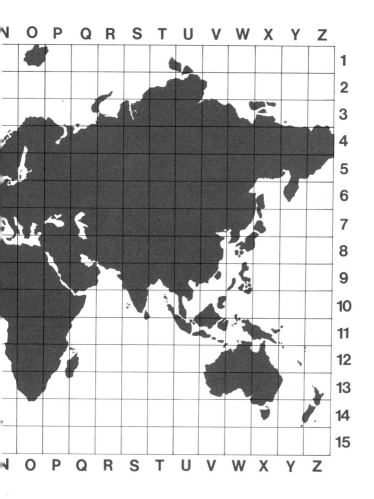

1
2
3
4
5
6
7
8
9
10
11
12
13
14
15

Ginger/Jamaica and Nigeria　　　　　　**H 9; N 10**

The dried rhizome (underground stem) of a plant belonging to the Ginger family. Believed to be native to south eastern Asia; cultivated in West Africa, West Indies, India, Ceylon, Indonesia, China and Japan.

Sold as whole and ground ginger.

Uses Pastries, biscuits, cakes, puddings, drinks and preserves.

Mace/Grenada　　　　　　**I 9**

(See **Nutmeg**.)

Obtained from an evergreen tree belonging to the Nutmeg family. Native to the Moluccas (Spice Islands); cultivated as well in Malaysia, West Indies and other tropical or sub-tropical climates.

Both mace and nutmeg are prepared from the fruit; mace is the aril (fruit fibre found inside the outer covering), nutmeg is the inner kernel. The fruit (nutmeg) is allowed to fall to the ground, then gathered quickly; the mace is carefully removed and the nutmegs and mace are dried separately — a slow, carefully controlled process. Mace has a fragrant, nutmeg-like odour.

Sold as ground mace.

Uses Meat pies, fish and vegetable dishes, cakes, biscuits, fruit puddings and chocolate dishes, preserves and pickles.
With **Nutmeg**, in Italian cookery, for savoury meat and white sauces.

Mustard Seed/England　　　　　　**M 6**

The whole, dried seeds of plants belonging to the Mustard family. Native to Europe and western temperate Asia; cultivated in many parts of the world. No perceptible odour, pungent taste.

Used in Blue Ribbon pickling spice (see page 23).

Uses Pickles and chutneys.

Nutmeg/Grenada　　　　　　**I 9**

(See **Mace**.)

Nutmeg has a characteristic odour and a slightly bitter taste.

Sold as whole and ground nutmeg.

Uses Some meat and vegetable dishes, pies, puddings, cakes, biscuits, fruit and beverages.
With **Mace**, in Italian cookery, for savoury meat and white sauces.

Paprika/Spain   M 7

The finely ground product of the large fruits (dried) of a capsicum plant belonging to the Potato family. Native to tropical America; cultivated in many tropical, sub-tropical and temperate regions. Varies from sweet to pungent in taste; colour ranges from brick red to bright red — the best quality.

Uses For flavouring and garnishing meat, egg, cheese and vegetable dishes, salads, soups.

Pepper/Brazil and Sarawak   J 11; V 10

The dried fruit of a vine belonging to the Pepper family. Native to the Malabar coast of southern India; cultivated in many tropical and sub-tropical parts of the world. The fruits are small, a dull green ripening to red; commonly called berries or pepper-corns. Rapid drying of slightly under-ripe berries produces black peppercorns. White pepper is prepared by soaking fully ripe berries and drying them slowly in the sun or by mechanical abrasion of dried black peppercorns.

Sold as black and white pepper, whole and ground.

Uses Universal use for seasoning and flavouring savoury dishes; black pepper gives a more pungent flavour than white; ground pepper deteriorates rapidly.
Whole pepper is used in pepper mills and dishes requiring long cooking and pickling.
Use ground white pepper instead of black for white sauces and pale coloured dishes.

Poppy Seed/Holland   N 6

The product of the Opium Poppy, a plant belonging to the Poppy family. Native to Asia; cultivated as well in Europe and North America. The 'blue' seed from the black poppy is more commonly employed. By the time the tiny seeds form, the plant has lost its opium content. Has a pleasing nut-like aroma and taste.

Uses Cakes, pastries, cookies, bread and confections.

Turmeric/India

The dried rhizome (underground stem) of a plant belonging to the Ginger family. Native to southern Asia and Indonesia; cultivated in tropical and sub-tropical regions. The rhizome is cured then polished. Has a pepper-like odour, bitter taste and yellow/orange colour.

Sold as ground turmeric.

Uses To flavour and colour meat, fish, rice and egg dishes, salad dressings, pickles, relishes, mustards, curries.

Seasonings and Flavourings

Blue Ribbon also market a range of seasonings and flavourings. The ingredients and uses of these are given below. For detailed information on the individual herbs and spices used in these blends, please refer to the preceding lists.

Apple Pie Spice

A blend of cassia cinnamon, nutmeg and sugar.

Uses Egg, milk and fruit puddings, scones and small cakes.

Barbecue Seasoning

A blend of sugar, salt, yeast, dextrose, paprika, white pepper, monosodium glutamate, onion powder, garlic powder, liquid smoke flavour.

Uses Hamburgers, casseroles, steaks, chops and vegetable dishes.

Bouquet Garni

Beef A blend of dried parsley, thyme, sweet basil and sage.

Lamb A blend of dried mint, rosemary, savory and sage.

Soup A blend of dried, ground parsley, sweet basil, thyme, marjoram and tarragon.

Uses Soups, stocks, sauces and the specified meat dishes. Bouquet garni for soup is used as well for poultry and veal.

Celery/Holland and Belgium   **M 6; N 6**

A plant belonging to the Carrot family. Native to southern Europe and northern Africa; cultivated in Europe, India, Japan and the U.S.A.

Sold as celery flakes.

Uses Soups, sauces, stocks, sea foods, vegetables, salads, eggs, meat loaf and poultry stuffing.

Celery Salt
(see Celery Seed)

Uses Fish, salads, salad dressings, soups, stews, egg and vegetable dishes.

Chilli Seasoning

A blend of paprika, salt, cayenne, cumin, oregano, garlic powder.

Uses Barbecue sauces, chilli con carne and other meat and poultry dishes, egg and cheese dishes.

Cream of Tartar/Italy and Spain   **M 7; N 7**
Bitartrate of potassium.

Uses Scones, cakes and puddings.

Curry Powder/India   **S 9/10**

A variety of formulae are used for curry powders—the spices often used are: cardamom seeds, chillies, coriander, cumin, fenugreek, ginger, mustard seed, pepper, turmeric. Salt is also added.

Blue Ribbon sell genuine Madras curry powder, blended in India to a secret recipe.

Uses Soups, sauces, curries and salad dressings.

Garlic/Egypt

The compound bulb of a plant belonging to the Lily family. The parts are called cloves. Native to Europe; cultivated almost universally. Strong, pungent flavour.

Sold as instant minced garlic, garlic powder, garlic pepper and garlic salt.

Uses Use instant minced garlic where chopped or minced garlic is required. Use the powder, pepper and salt in any dish requiring garlic flavour such as soups, sauces, stocks, salad dressings.

Italian Seasoning

A blend of oregano, rosemary, marjoram, savory, sage, thyme and sweet basil.

Uses Meat and poultry dishes, soups, sauces, salad dressings, stuffings, pasta and pizza dishes.

Meat Tenderiser

A blend of salt, dextrose, wheat flour, papain and calcium silicate.

Uses To make steaks, chops, chicken and roasts more tender and flavourful.

Mixed Fine Herbs

A blend of dried parsley, sweet basil and oregano.

Uses Soups, sauces, salads, meat, egg, cheese and tomato dishes.

Mixed Spice

A blend of cassia cinnamon, allspice, cloves, ginger, nutmeg, anise seed, caraway and sugar.

Uses Meat dishes, cakes, biscuits, pies, fruits, hot puddings and drinks.

Mushroom Powder/East European　　　N 6; O 6

There are many varieties of edible fungi; Blue Ribbon use Boletus Edulis, which is cleaned after picking, artificially dehydrated then powdered.

Uses Soups, sauces, gravies, casseroles, meat loaf and dishes requiring mushroom flavour.

Onion/Egypt　　　O 8

The bulb of a plant belonging to the Lily family. Believed to have originated in the eastern Mediterranean and Middle East; cultivated widely in temperate and tropical regions.

Sold as onion flakes, instant minced onion, onion powder and onion salt.

Uses Use onion flakes and instant minced onion instead of raw onion. Salt and powder are a convenient way of adding onion flavour to dishes.

Parmesan/Italy　　　N 7

A large, exceptionally hard cheese made from skimmed milk in the district of Parma, Italy. Usually available grated; has a strong flavour; ideal as a cooking cheese.

Uses Soups, cheese sauce, Italian and pasta dishes, cheese pastries.

Pickling Spice

A uniquely English mixture, varying in formula. Blue Ribbon's is: coriander seed, mustard seed, cassia cinnamon, bay leaves, chillies, ginger, black pepper, cloves, dill, caraway seed.

Uses Pickling meat, vegetables, eggs, relishes and chutneys.

Poultry Seasoning

A blend of savory, sage, thyme, oregano, ground black pepper, marjoram, ginger, cloves, allspice.

Uses Stuffing for meats and poultry, meat balls, meat loaf and dumplings to go with meat.

Salad Seasoning

A blend of salt, sugar, lactose, mustard, wheat flour, onion powder, monosodium glutamate, turmeric, black pepper, fenugreek, paprika, garlic powder, spice extractive, tarragon, cumin seed.

Uses Enhances the flavour of salads and salad dressings, cooked and raw vegetables.

Steak Spice

A blend of coriander seed, celery seed, marjoram, garlic powder, ground black pepper, onion powder.

Uses Steaks, chops, stews, hamburgers and meat loaf.

How to use Herbs and Spices in cooking

Used imaginatively, herbs and spices can add excitement to cooking and transform everyday food into tempting dishes. As a guide to using the many varieties of herbs and spices available, here are some points to consider:

1 *Spice* should not be confused with *hot;* most spices are mild and add subtle flavour to a dish when used sparingly.

2 Measure each herb and spice carefully to give the desired flavour; too much can ruin the flavour especially when several herbs and spices are used in the same recipe.

3 Experiment in the use of herbs and spices and learn from experience. When you know what is good with one type of food, try to think of other types of food with which to use a particular flavour. When changing the herb or spice in a particular recipe, do not alter the other ingredients.

4 Try smelling the jars of herbs and spices to give you an indication of the flavour you can expect.

5 If you enjoy the flavour of herbs and spices in food, buy a herb or spice you have not used before, say every month,

and you will soon have a good selection with which to experiment.

6 All herbs and spices gradually lose their aroma and flavouring properties, so check the jars from time to time and discard as necessary to ensure you will always be able to produce tasty dishes.

Storage

1 Remember to screw the caps on tightly after use to retain the aroma and flavouring properties of the herbs and spices.

2 Jars should be kept in a dry place to keep the contents in top condition.

3 Remember also to store the jars in the coolest part of the kitchen, away from the heat of the cooker, direct sunlight, or any other source of heat.

Recipe notes

All the recipes in the succeeding chapters have been tested with Blue Ribbon products. The quality of herbs, spices and season-ings can vary so if brands other than Blue Ribbon are used, you may not get the same results. Where 'pepper' is given as an ingredient in a recipe, Blue Ribbon ground white or black pepper, or alternatively, whole peppercorns ground in a mill, may be used, unless one variety is specifically stated.

All spoon measurements throughout the book are LEVEL spoon measurements measured in British Standard Imperial spoons.

All other measurements are Imperial weights and measures.

Beginnings

Country Soup
Serves 4

1 large onion, chopped	1 teaspoon bouquet garni
1 oz. butter	for soup
8 oz. carrots	$\frac{3}{4}$ pint water
$\frac{1}{4}$ small white cabbage	4 oz. pasta shapes
2 chicken stock cubes,	salt
dissolved in 1 pint water	pepper

Melt butter and cook onions gently for 2−3 minutes without browning. Cut carrots into $\frac{1}{2}$ inch thin strips, chop cabbage roughly and add to onion. Cook for 3−4 minutes stirring occasionally. Pour in chicken stock and add bouquet garni. Simmer for 30 minutes. Add $\frac{3}{4}$ pint water, bring to boil and add pasta shapes. Simmer for a further 15 minutes until pasta is just cooked. Check seasoning.

Serve with grated cheese and hot French bread.

Creamed Mushroom and Corn Soup
Serves 4

6 oz. mushrooms, sliced	pepper
1 onion, sliced	2 teaspoons mushroom
1 chicken stock cube,	powder
dissolved in $\frac{1}{2}$ pint water	$\frac{1}{4}$ teaspoon ground mace
1 oz. butter	8 oz. packet frozen sweet
1 oz. flour	corn
$\frac{1}{2}$ pint milk	1 egg yolk
1 teaspoon salt	$\frac{1}{4}$ pint single cream

Simmer mushroom and onion together in the chicken stock for 15 minutes. Reserve a few mushroom slices for garnish, reduce remaining mixture to a purée. Melt butter in a large saucepan, stir in flour and blend in milk. Heat, stirring until thickened. Add mushroom purée, salt, pepper, mushroom powder, mace and sweet corn. Cook for a further 15 minutes over very gentle heat. Just before serving beat yolk into cream. Remove soup from heat and add cream, stirring continuously. Do not allow the soup to boil after adding the cream. Add mushroom slices and serve.

Minted Pea Soup
Serves 4

¾ pint water

2 teaspoons mint

1 chicken stock cube

1 lb. peas, fresh or frozen

salt

pepper

2 - 3 tablespoons single cream

Place water, mint and stock cube into saucepan and simmer gently for 5 minutes. Add peas, bring to boil and continue simmering for 7 minutes. Reduce soup to a purée and return to saucepan and bring to boil. Check seasoning. Remove from heat and stir in cream. Serve at once. An extra tablespoon of cream may be carefully poured into the centre of the soup for garnish. Serve with melba toast or gristicks.

Rich Onion Soup
Serves 6

2 oz. lard or dripping

1 lb. onions, peeled and finely chopped

1 oz. flour

2 chicken stock cubes, dissolved in 1½ pints water

2 teaspoons tomato purée

½ teaspoon savory

salt

pepper

Melt lard or dripping in a pan. Fry onions slowly in fat until beginning to brown. Blend in flour, cook gently until beginning to brown. Add stock and stir until smooth. Add remaining ingredients, cover and simmer 30 – 40 minutes.

Asparagus Soup
Serves 4

1 oz. butter
1 oz. flour
1 chicken stock cube,
dissolved in ½ pint water
¼ pint milk
salt

pepper
pinch of sugar
½ teaspoon chervil
10½ oz. can cut asparagus
spears
few drops green colouring

Melt butter in pan, add flour and cook 1 minute. Blend in
stock and milk then bring to boiling point, stirring. Add
seasoning, sugar and chervil. Cut off asparagus tips and keep
for garnish. Add rest of asparagus and liquid to pan. Cover and
simmer 10 minutes. Reduce soup to a purée then return to pan
and reheat, adding a few drops of green colouring if necessary.
Garnish with reserved asparagus tips.

Spinach Cream Soup
Serves 4

½ pint milk
1 tablespoon onion flakes
6 peppercorns
1 whole bay leaf
1 oz. butter
1 oz. flour
1 beef stock cube,
dissolved in ¾ pint water

12 oz. packet frozen leaf
spinach, thawed
salt
pepper
pinch nutmeg
5 oz. carton soured cream

Put milk in pan with onion, peppercorns and bay leaf. Bring
slowly to boiling point then remove from heat and infuse for
20 minutes. Melt butter in clean pan, add flour and cook
1 minute. Blend in strained milk and bring to boiling point,
stirring. Add remaining ingredients, except cream. Simmer 5 –
10 minutes. Reduce soup to a purée then return to pan.
Check seasoning and stir in soured cream. Reheat almost to
simmering point but do not boil.

Home Made Tomato Soup
Serves 4

$\frac{1}{2}$ oz. butter
1 onion, sliced
$\frac{1}{2}$ oz. flour
2 chicken stock cubes, dissolved in $1\frac{1}{4}$ pints water
$\frac{1}{4}$ teaspoon ground mace
1 whole clove
$\frac{1}{2}$ teaspoon salt

pepper
$\frac{1}{2}$ teaspoon caster sugar
1 teaspoon paprika
$\frac{1}{2}$ teaspoon marjoram
1 whole bay leaf
$\frac{1}{4}$ teaspoon parsley
14 oz. can tomatoes

Melt butter in a pan, add onion and fry slowly until soft. Blend in flour, then stock and bring to boiling point, stirring. Add rest of ingredients, cover and simmer 30 minutes. Remove bay leaf. Re-boil and check seasoning before serving.

Chilled Avocado Soup
Serves 6

3 ripe avocado pears
2 × 15 oz. cans consommé
5 oz. carton soured cream
salt

pepper
1 tablespoon lemon juice
1 teaspoon chives

Remove stones from pears, scoop out flesh and reduce to a purée. Heat consommé in a pan until just simmering. Remove from heat and blend with avocado purée. Add soured cream, seasoning, lemon juice and chives. Refrigerate in covered plastic container. Expect mixture to discolour slightly on top. Stir well before ladling into individual soup bowls.

Spiced Croûtons
To serve with soups.
Serves 4

4 slices of bread, $\frac{1}{2}$ inch thick
2 tablespoons oil
1 oz. butter

salt
pepper
1 teaspoon ground mace

Remove crusts and cut bread into $\frac{1}{2}$ inch cubes. Fry in oil and butter until golden brown. Remove and drain on kitchen paper. Sprinkle with salt, pepper and mace making sure that the croûtons are evenly covered.

Kipper Pâté
Serves 6

10 oz. frozen kipper fillets, thawed

marinade

4½ tablespoons salad oil
3 tablespoons cider vinegar
small pinch ground
black pepper

½ teaspoon made mustard
½ teaspoon mixed fine herbs
¼ teaspoon garlic powder
1 hard-boiled egg, chopped

Dip kipper fillets in boiling water for 1 minute then peel off skins. Mix together marinade ingredients, except egg. Soak fillets in marinade in a cold place for 24 hours, turning occasionally. Pound fillets and marinade until smooth. Add egg and mix well. Turn into a small serving dish and chill before serving. Serve with hot toast, butter and lemon wedges.

Herb Cheese Pâté
Serves 4 - 6

8 oz. well-matured Cheddar cheese, finely grated
¼ pint single cream
4 tablespoons sweet sherry
1 teaspoon ground sage
1 teaspoon chervil

1 teaspoon parsley
1 teaspoon thyme
½ teaspoon onion powder
1 oz. butter
½ teaspoon salt
sprigs of parsley

Mix together all ingredients except parsley in top of a double boiler or in a basin over a pan of hot water on a gentle heat and stir until thoroughly mixed and creamy. Turn into 4 – 6 ramekins or small pots and allow to cool. Leave at least 12 hours before eating. Garnish with parsley sprigs.

Serve with crackers or hot toast.

Chicken Liver Pâté
Serves 4 - 6

4 oz. butter

1 medium onion, finely chopped

8 oz. chicken livers

1 whole bay leaf

$\frac{1}{4}$ teaspoon thyme

$\frac{1}{2}$ teaspoon parsley

$\frac{1}{4}$ teaspoon garlic powder

$\frac{1}{2}$ teaspoon salt

$\frac{1}{4}$ teaspoon ground black pepper

1 tablespoon brandy

Melt 1 oz. of the butter in a saucepan, add onion and cook until just beginning to brown. Add chicken livers, herbs and seasonings and fry over a medium heat for 4 minutes. Cool. Reduce mixture to a smooth paste. Cream remaining butter and gradually beat in liver mixture. Add brandy and extra seasoning if necessary. Serve with hot toast.

Spiced Grapefruit and Orange Cocktail
Serves 4

3 large oranges

2 small grapefruit

sugar

1 teaspoon ground ginger

4 morello or glacé cherries

Cut all peel and pith from oranges and grapefruit with a sharp knife. Remove segments by cutting either side of sections. Mix orange and grapefruit segments together and divide between 4 individual dishes. Sprinkle with sugar and ground ginger. Place a cherry in the centre of each dish.

Iced Jellied Eggs
Serves 6

15 oz. can consommé

$\frac{1}{2}$ oz. powdered gelatine

6 small eggs

4 oz. can pâté de foie truffe

$\frac{1}{4}$ teaspoon rubbed sage

Put consommé in pan with gelatine. Heat gently, without boiling, until gelatine has dissolved, then cool. Soft boil eggs for 6 minutes. Remove shells carefully, then put eggs in bowl of cold water. Pour $\frac{1}{4}$ inch of consommé into 6 individual ramekins then leave in a cold place to set. Put an egg in each ramekin and pour over more consommé to cover. Leave again until set. Blend pâté with sage, spread a layer of pâté on top of each ramekin and leave in a cold place until needed. Just before serving turn out. Serve with warm French bread.

Avocado Mayonnaise Cocktail
Serves 4

Mayonnaise

1 egg yolk
¼ teaspoon French mustard
¼ teaspoon garlic powder
¼ teaspoon salt

1 teaspoon paprika
¼ pint oil
1 - 2 tablespoons wine vinegar
2 ripe avocado pears

Place egg yolk in a bowl and beat well with mustard, garlic powder, salt and paprika. Gradually whisk in oil, a few drops at a time, until mixture begins to thicken. Add 2 teaspoons of vinegar and continue whisking in oil. Stir in remaining vinegar until desired consistency and flavour is reached.

Peel avocado pears and remove stones. Cut into ½ inch dice and place in a dish. Cover with the mayonnaise and sprinkle with more paprika.

Spring Aioli
Serves 6

1 lb. 8 oz. mixed prepared
vegetables, e.g. new
potatoes, baby
turnips, new carrots,
fresh peas
spring onions
tomatoes, skinned and
quartered

Aioli (Garlic Mayonnaise)
1 teaspoon garlic powder
3 egg yolks
$\frac{1}{3}$ pint vegetable oil
$\frac{1}{2}$ teaspoon salt
$\frac{1}{8}$ teaspoon ground white
pepper
2 tablespoons lemon juice

Blend garlic powder and egg yolks in a bowl. Gradually
whisk in oil. Stir in seasoning and lemon juice. Cook root
vegetables and peas separately in usual way. Turn into a
colander, rinse with cold water and drain thoroughly. Arrange
vegetables on a serving dish in separate piles. Serve with
aioli sauce.

Eggs in Minted Soured Cream
Serves 4

1 teaspoon mint
5 oz. carton soured cream
4 eggs, hard-boiled and
shelled

4 lettuce leaves
4 lemon slices

Stir mint into soured cream at least 2 hours before serving.
Strain through a sieve to remove most of the mint. Cut hard-
boiled eggs into quarters and arrange neatly in a dish. Cover
with soured cream and garnish with lettuce leaves and twists
of lemon.

Salami Italian-style
Serves 4

Vinaigrette
$\frac{1}{2}$ teaspoon Italian seasoning
1 tablespoon oil
1 tablespoon wine vinegar

salt
pepper
16 slices Italian salami
2 large tomatoes, sliced

Blend together ingredients for vinaigrette at least 1 hour
before serving. Remove skin from salami and arrange slices
in a dish with tomato slices. Cover with vinaigrette.

Tomatoes in Oregano Vinaigrette
Serves 4

Vinaigrette
$\frac{1}{2}$ teaspoon ground oregano
1 tablespoon oil
1 tablespoon wine vinegar

salt
pepper
6 tomatoes, sliced

Mix together all ingredients for vinaigrette 1 hour before serving. Layer sliced tomatoes neatly in a dish. Pour over vinaigrette.

Button Mushrooms with Dill
Serves 4

1 teaspoon dill seed
4 tablespoons water
4 tablespoons white wine or dry sherry
salt

pepper
8 oz. button mushrooms, washed
1 tablespoon parsley, finely chopped

Place dill seed, water, wine, salt and pepper in a saucepan with a tight fitting lid. Heat gently for 5 minutes. Strain and discard dill seed. Return wine infusion to pan, add mushrooms, cover with lid and poach gently for 5 minutes. Chill. Arrange mushrooms in a dish and pour over remaining liquor. Garnish with chopped parsley.

Egg and Tomato Mayonnaise
Serves 4

$\frac{1}{4}$ pint thick mayonnaise
2 tablespoons soured cream
$\frac{1}{2}$ teaspoon mixed fine herbs
$\frac{1}{4}$ teaspoon tarragon leaves
pinch cayenne

4 large tomatoes
4 hard-boiled eggs, shelled and sliced
bunch of watercress

Mix mayonnaise, soured cream, herbs and cayenne together. Leave to infuse for at least 4 hours or overnight in a refrigerator. When ready to serve place tomatoes, stalk ends down, and make 5 cuts in each to about three quarters of the way down. Insert thin slices of egg between each slice. Serve on bed of watercress with the mayonnaise spooned over the top.

French Dressed Artichokes
Serves 6

French Dressing

1 teaspoon caster sugar
½ teaspoon salt
⅛ teaspoon ground black pepper
1 teaspoon chives
5 tablespoons olive oil
2 tablespoons wine vinegar
¼ teaspoon sweet basil

6 firm tomatoes, skinned
2 × 12 oz. cans globe artichoke hearts, drained
1 tablespoon chopped parsley

Blend together all ingredients for dressing. Slice tomatoes thinly and arrange on individual plates. Arrange artichokes on top, spoon over dressing. Leave in cold place until just before serving. Scatter with parsley and serve with thinly sliced brown bread and butter.

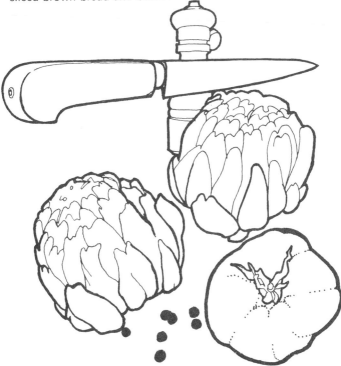

Ox Tongues Vinaigrette
Serves 4 – 6

1 lb. can ox tongue

Sauce Vinaigrette
$\frac{1}{2}$ teaspoon garlic salt
$\frac{1}{8}$ teaspoon ground black pepper
2 teaspoons caster sugar
1 teaspoon French mustard

8 tablespoons vegetable oil
4 tablespoons white wine vinegar
1 teaspoon mint
1 tablespoon parsley

Remove all jelly from tongue and cut meat in thin slices. Arrange on a serving dish, cover and put in refrigerator. Melt jelly in a pan, leave to cool. Make vinaigrette sauce by blending all ingredients together, then add molted jelly. Spoon over tongue.

Avocado and Oregano Dip
Serves 6 – 8

2 ripe avocado pears
6 tablespoons thick mayonnaise
1 teaspoon made mustard
2 teaspoons caster sugar

2 teaspoons lemon juice
$\frac{1}{2}$ teaspoon ground oregano
salt
pepper
green colouring (optional)

Cut pears in half and remove stones, scoop out flesh and purée in a blender with mayonnaise, mustard, sugar, lemon juice and oregano, or mash together with a fork. Add seasoning as required and a few drops of green colouring if necessary. Turn into serving bowl and cover until required.

Serve with small crackers, potato crisps or sticks of raw vegetables, such as celery or carrot.

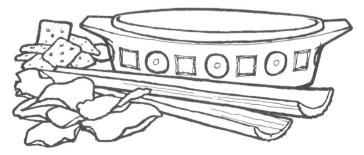

Parmesan Dip
Serves 6

6 oz. soft cream cheese or curd cheese

3 tablespoons single cream

$\frac{1}{4}$ teaspoon garlic powder

$\frac{1}{4}$ teaspoon ground white pepper

2 tablespoons Parmesan

Blend cream cheese with cream until smooth. Add remaining ingredients and mix well. Cover and leave overnight before serving to allow flavours to blend. Serve with small crackers, potato crisps or raw vegetable sticks.

Italian Cheese Mouthfuls
Serves 6

2 large slices white bread, $\frac{1}{4}$ inch thick

oil or fat for frying

8 oz. cream cheese

1 oz. softened butter

2 tablespoons Parmesan

salt

pepper

paprika

Remove crusts from bread. Cut each slice in 9 squares. Fry in oil or fat until golden brown then drain on kitchen paper.

Mix cream cheese in a bowl with butter, and add Parmesan and plenty of seasoning. Put mixture into a large piping bag fitted with a rose nozzle and pipe mixture onto croûtes.

Sprinkle a little paprika on top.

Mild Curried Eggs
Serves 4

6 small eggs, hard-boiled

1 oz. butter

1 tablespoon mayonnaise

1 teaspoon curry powder

1 teaspoon mango chutney juice

salt

pepper

2 gherkins, sliced

bunch of watercress

Cut shelled eggs in half widthways. Cut a small slice from bottom of each half so they will stand up. Remove and sieve yolks. Blend in butter, mayonnaise, curry powder and mango juice. Add seasoning to taste. Spoon mixture into egg 'shells' with a teaspoon. Decorate with sliced gherkin. Serve on a bed of watercress.

Herrings with Spiced Cream and Cucumber
Serves 6

Cucumber Salad

3 tablespoons salad oil
2 tablespoons water
2 tablespoons vinegar
2 teaspoons caster sugar
$\frac{1}{4}$ teaspoon dill seed
$\frac{1}{4}$ teaspoon salt
$\frac{1}{2}$ cucumber, thinly sliced

Spiced Cream

2 teaspoons lemon juice
1 teaspoon mustard powder
2 teaspoons caster sugar

1 teaspoon instant minced onion
$\frac{1}{4}$ teaspoon salt
$\frac{1}{8}$ teaspoon ground black pepper
1 teaspoon chives
$\frac{1}{4}$ pint double cream, lightly whipped

6 oz. can herring fillets, drained
1 tablespoon chopped parsley

Blend together all salad ingredients except cucumber. Pour mixture over cucumber, leave to marinate about 30 minutes. Mix together lemon juice, mustard, sugar, onion, salt, pepper and chives and blend until smooth. Fold in cream.

Half an hour before serving, drain most of the liquid from cucumber, arrange overlapping slices on large flat dish. Arrange herring fillets on top of cucumber. Top with spiced cream, scatter with chopped parsley.

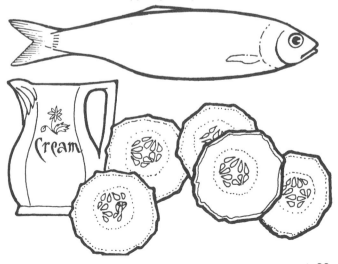

Fish dishes

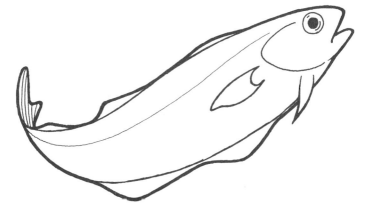

Baked Cod Steaks with Orange

Serves 4

Oven temperature 350 deg. F., Gas No. 4

4 medium-sized cod steaks
juice of $\frac{1}{2}$ lemon
1 teaspoon fennel seed
salt
pepper
1 orange, peeled and cut into 4 rings

small onion, cut into thin rings
1 oz. butter
$\frac{1}{2}$ oz. flour
$\frac{1}{4}$ pint milk

Wash cod and arrange in a well-buttered ovenproof dish. Sprinkle with lemon juice and fennel seed and season well. Place a slice of orange on each steak with onion rings. Dot with $\frac{1}{2}$ oz. of the butter and cover with foil. Bake at 350 deg. F., Gas No. 4, for 15 minutes. Melt remaining $\frac{1}{2}$ oz. butter in a saucepan, stir in flour and cook for 1 minute. Gradually add milk and cook until thickened. When fish is cooked add liquor from baking dish to sauce, reheat and check seasoning. To serve either pour sauce around fish or serve separately.

Cod Steaks with Basil

Serves 4

Oven temperature 425 deg. F., Gas No. 7

4 cod steaks
$10\frac{1}{2}$ oz. can condensed mushroom soup
1 teaspoon sweet basil

3 tomatoes
2 oz. Cheddar cheese, grated
sprigs of parsley

Place cod steaks in shallow ovenproof dish approximately 8" x 8" x $1\frac{1}{2}$". Spoon soup over each cod steak and sprinkle with sweet basil. Skin tomatoes and slice. Arrange on top of the soup and fish. Sprinkle with grated cheese and bake at 425 deg. F., Gas No. 7, for 30 minutes. Garnish with sprigs of parsley.

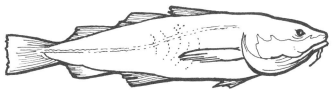

Cod With Lemon Sauce

Serves 4

Oven temperature 325 deg. F., Gas No. 3

4 cod steaks
1 small onion, sliced
1 whole bay leaf
6 black peppercorns
1/4 teaspoon mixed fine herbs
1/8 pint dry cider
thinly peeled rind of 1/2 lemon

Sauce
1/4 pint fish liquor
1 tablespoon cornflour
juice of 1/2 lemon
1/4 pint milk
2 egg yolks
salt
pepper
sprigs of parsley

Put cod in a shallow 2 pint ovenproof dish. Add other ingredients, cover and bake at 325 deg. F., Gas No. 3, for about 20 minutes. Remove skin and bones, transfer fish to a serving dish and keep hot. Strain cooking liquor into a measuring jug and make up to 1/4 pint with water. Blend fish liquor in a pan with cornflour and lemon juice. Bring to boiling point, stirring, and simmer 2 minutes. Blend together milk and egg yolks. Add to sauce and bring to simmering point but do not boil. Check seasoning, pour sauce over fish and garnish with parsley.

Egg and Parsley Stuffed Herrings

Serves 4

Oven temperature 375 deg. F., Gas No. 5

4 whole boned herrings	½ teaspoon thyme
salt	1 hard-boiled egg,
pepper	finely chopped
	½ teaspoon salt
Stuffing	pepper
2 oz. white breadcrumbs	milk to mix
1 small onion, finely	½ oz. butter
chopped	1 lemon
1 tablespoon parsley	

Open fish out flat and season well.

Place breadcrumbs, onion, parsley, thyme, hard-boiled egg, salt and pepper into a bowl. Add enough milk to bind stuffing. Divide equally into four, use to stuff herrings and fold each fish over. Place in a lightly buttered ovenproof dish, dot with butter, cover with foil and bake at 375 deg. F., Gas No. 5, for 30 minutes. Serve garnished with wedges of lemon.

Mackerel With Gooseberry Sauce

Serves 4

4 mackerel	*Gooseberry Sauce*
2 tablespoons fine oatmeal	8 oz. gooseberries
½ teaspoon salt	2 tablespoons water
½ oz. butter	½ oz. butter
	¼ teaspoon ground nutmeg

Cut off mackerel heads and clean fish thoroughly. Remove tails and fins then wash in cold water. Drain and dry on kitchen paper. Mix together oatmeal and salt. Use to coat mackerel. Melt butter in a heavy pan, add mackerel and fry about 15 – 20 minutes, turning once. Put gooseberries in a pan with water, butter and nutmeg. Cover and simmer until soft. Reduce to a purée then reheat before serving with mackerel.

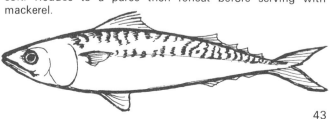

Halibut With Shrimp Sauce
Serves 4

4 halibut steaks
$\frac{1}{2}$ pint water
thinly peeled rind and juice
of $\frac{1}{2}$ lemon
1 whole bay leaf
$\frac{1}{2}$ teaspoon Italian seasoning
6 white peppercorns
1 tablepoon onion flakes

$\frac{1}{2}$ teaspoon salt

Shrimp Sauce
2 oz. butter
juice of $\frac{1}{2}$ lemon
2 oz. peeled shrimps
1 tablespoon chopped
parsley

Put halibut in shallow pan with other ingredients. Cover and simmer gently about 15 minutes until fish just flakes. Remove fish from pan, put on a serving dish and keep hot. Melt butter for sauce in a pan. Add lemon juice, shrimps and parsley. Pour sauce over fish and serve.

Baked Lemon Sole
Serves 4
Oven temperature 325 deg. F., Gas No. 3

4 lemon soles
3 oz. Port Salut cheese,
finely diced
2 tomatoes, skinned,
de-pipped and chopped
1 tablespoon parsley
1 teaspoon fennel seed

2 oz. fresh white
breadcrumbs
$\frac{1}{2}$ oz. butter
$\frac{1}{2}$ teaspoon salt
$\frac{1}{4}$ teaspoon ground black
pepper

Have heads and fins removed from soles by fishmonger. Put fish, white side uppermost, on table. With a sharp knife cut through to backbone from top to tail. Ease flesh away from each side of backbone, turning flesh back. Mix cheese, tomato, parsley and fennel seed together. Fry breadcrumbs in butter until golden then add to cheese mixture with seasoning. Use to fill centre space in fish. Put on a buttered baking tray, cover loosely with foil and bake at 325 deg. F., Gas No. 3, for 20 minutes.

Sole with Creamed Mushrooms
Serves 4

1½ oz. butter

1 medium onion, finely chopped

4 sole fillets

1 teaspoon bouquet garni for lamb

½ chicken stock cube, dissolved in ½ pint water

¼ pint white wine

4 oz. button mushrooms, sliced

1 oz. flour

2 tablespoons double cream

salt

pepper

Melt ½ oz. of the butter in frying pan, add onion and cook gently for 2−3 minutes. Meanwhile cut each sole fillet in half lengthways and fold each into three. Add bouquet garni, chicken stock, wine, mushrooms and sole fillets to pan, cover and poach for 10 minutes until sole is cooked. Remove sole and keep hot on serving dish. Strain cooking liquor. Reserve mushrooms.

Melt remaining butter in a small pan, add flour and cook for 1 minute. Gradually add cooking liquor and bring to the boil, stirring. Add mushrooms. Remove from heat and stir in cream. Check seasoning. Pour sauce over sole fillets and serve. Pour sauce over sole fillets and serve.

Bo'suns Stew

Serves 6 – 8

3 lb. fish to include
mackerel
plaice
whiting
rock salmon
$2\frac{1}{2}$ pints water
3 tablespoons olive oil
1 leek, sliced
5 oz. can prawns, drained
4 tablespoons onion flakes

4 tomatoes, skinned and
chopped
$\frac{1}{4}$ teaspoon fennel seed
$\frac{1}{8}$ teaspoon turmeric
$\frac{1}{4}$ teaspoon ground bay
leaves
2 teaspoons parsley
1 teaspoon salt
pepper
6 – 8 slices French bread

Get fishmonger to fillet and skin mackerel, plaice, whiting and rock salmon. Keep skin and bones for stock. Put skin and bones in a pan with $2\frac{1}{2}$ pints water, bring to boiling point, simmer 20 minutes then strain off fish liquor. Heat oil in a large pan, add leek and fry slowly until golden. Add fish, cut in chunks, and cook gently for 5 minutes, then add 2 pints fish liquor and all remaining ingredients except bread. Simmer about 10 minutes until fish is cooked. Leave for at least 2 hours before serving. Reheat and check seasoning. Put French bread in a tureen and pour over fish stew.

Haddock Mayonnaise

Serves 4

1 lb. haddock fillets
$\frac{1}{4}$ pint water
juice of $\frac{1}{2}$ lemon
salt
pepper
1 tablespoon chopped
parsley

6 tablespoons thick
mayonnaise
2 tablespoons fish liquor,
strained
$\frac{1}{2}$ teaspoon savory
paprika

Put fish in a shallow pan with water, cover and simmer 10 minutes. Remove fish from pan, discard skin and bones and flake fish. Add lemon juice and seasoning. When cold blend in remaining ingredients except paprika. Chill in covered container. Serve on a bed of green salad, sprinkled with a little paprika.

Bream Fish Pie

Serves 4

Oven temperature 325 deg. F., Gas No. 3

1 oz. butter
1 lb. 8 oz. bream fillet
1 tablespoon onion flakes
6 white peppercorns
$\frac{1}{4}$ teaspoon thyme
1 cooking apple, peeled, cored and sliced
$\frac{1}{4}$ pint dry cider
$\frac{1}{2}$ oz. flour

4 oz. button mushrooms, sliced
2 teaspoons parsley
salt
pepper
$7\frac{1}{2}$ oz. packet frozen puff pastry, thawed
egg for glazing

Butter a shallow 3 pint ovenproof dish with $\frac{1}{2}$ oz. of the butter. Put in fish, onion, peppercorns, thyme, apple and cider. Cover and cook at 325 deg. F., Gas No. 3, for 20 minutes or until fish flakes easily. Flake fish and put on one side with apple slices. Strain fish liquor into a measuring jug and make up to $\frac{1}{4}$ pint with water. Melt remaining butter in pan, blend in flour and cook 1 minute. Blend in fish liquor and bring to boiling point, stirring. Add mushrooms and cook 3 minutes, then stir in parsley and seasoning. Add fish and apple to sauce, turn into 2 pint pie dish and leave to cool. Roll out pastry to fit dish and cover in usual way. Brush with beaten egg and bake at 425 deg. F., Gas No. 7, for about 25 minutes until golden brown.

Bombay Prawn Curry
Serves 4

4 large onions, sliced
2 tablespoons oil
1 teaspoon ground ginger
1 teaspoon garlic powder
$\frac{1}{8}$ teaspoon chilli seasoning
$\frac{1}{4}$ teaspoon ground mace
$\frac{1}{2}$ teaspoon turmeric
$\frac{1}{4}$ pint water
1 tablespoon tomato purée

1 lb. peeled prawns
4 lemon slices
4 fresh green chillies, cut in
half lengthways, and seeded
salt
pepper

Fry onions in a large saucepan in oil until golden brown. Add ginger, garlic, chilli seasoning, mace and turmeric. Cook for a further 10 minutes, stirring continuously. Add water, tomato purée, prawns, lemon slices and chillies. Simmer for 10 minutes. Season to taste. Serve with boiled rice, chapattis and Bombay duck.

Salmon Fish Cakes
Serves 4

7 oz. can grade 2 salmon
1 lb. potatoes, peeled
1 oz. butter
1 tablespoon parsley
$\frac{1}{4}$ teaspoon dill seed
1 egg, beaten
salt
pepper

Coating
2 tablespoons milk
flour
browned breadcrumbs
lard or oil for deep frying

Discard skin and bones of salmon. Reserve juice and flake fish. Boil potatoes in usual way then strain and mash with butter. Mix with salmon, parsley, dill seed and half of the egg. Add a little salmon juice to bind. Check seasoning then divide mixture into 8 pieces and shape into cakes. Blend milk with remaining half of egg. Toss cakes in flour then coat with egg and crumbs. Fry in hot lard or oil until golden brown. Drain on kitchen paper before serving.

Soused Herrings with Marjoram
Serves 4

Oven temperature 325 deg. F., Gas No. 3

4 whole herrings, boned and filleted	$\frac{1}{2}$ teaspoon ground mace
salt	6 black peppercorns
pepper	3 whole bay leaves
$\frac{1}{2}$ pint vinegar	$\frac{1}{2}$ teaspoon marjoram
$\frac{1}{4}$ pint water	

Season fillets and roll up starting at tail and with skin out-side. Place close together in shallow ovenproof dish. Pour over mixture of vinegar, water, mace, black peppercorns, bay leaves and marjoram. Cover with lid or foil and bake at 325 deg. F., Gas No. 3, for $1\frac{1}{4}$ hours. When cooked leave to cool. Drain and serve cold with salads.

Rollmops
Makes 12

4 oz. salt	1 tablespoon pickling spice
2 pints water	1 onion, finely sliced
12 small herrings, boned and cleaned	$\frac{1}{2}$ teaspoon crushed chillies
1 pint distilled malt vinegar	1 whole bay leaf

Mix salt and water together. Add herrings to brine. Leave 2 hours. Put vinegar and pickling spice in a pan, bring slowly to boiling point. Remove from heat. Leave to infuse 30 minutes. Strain and cool.

Roll up herrings, skin side outside and secure with half a cocktail stick. Pack into a wide-necked jar with a few onion rings between, add chillies and bay leaf. Cover with spiced vinegar. Cover with a lid, leave 5 to 6 days in a cold place before using. Herrings preserved in this way will keep 4 weeks in a refrigerator.

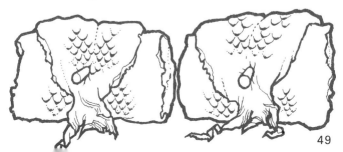

49

Meat dishes

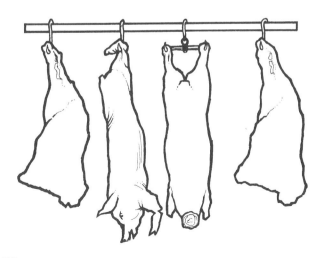

Beef Goulash with Caraway Seed Dumplings

Serves 4

Oven temperature 350 deg. F., Gas No. 4

1 large onion, finely chopped
1 oz. butter
1 tablespoon oil
1 lb. 8 oz. stewing beef
1½ oz. seasoned flour
1 beef stock cube, dissolved in ½ pint water
¼ pint red wine
2 tablespoons paprika
salt
pepper

Dumplings
6 oz. self-raising flour
1 teaspoon salt
2 oz. suet, finely shredded
grated rind of ½ lemon
2 teaspoons caraway seed
2 tablespoons water

Melt butter with oil in a frying pan and cook onion gently for about 5 minutes. Remove and keep on one side. Cut meat into ½ inch cubes and toss in seasoned flour. Brown thoroughly on all sides in pan. Stir in any remaining seasoned flour, cook for 2 minutes and remove from heat. Add onion, stock, wine and paprika and bring to the boil for 2 – 3 minutes, stirring continuously. Transfer to a 4 pint ovenproof casserole. Cover with lid and bake at 350 deg. F., Gas No. 4, for 2 hours until meat is tender. After 1½ hours stir goulash well and season if necessary. Add prepared dumplings and continue cooking for ½ hour.

Dumplings Sift flour and salt, add suet, grated lemon rind and caraway seed and mix together thoroughly. Gradually add water and bind to form a stiff dough. Divide into eight equal portions and roll each piece to a smooth ball.

Beef Olives

Serves 4

Oven temperature 350 deg. F., Gas No. 4

1 lb. 8 oz. topside of beef cut into 8 thin slices

salt

pepper

1 medium onion, finely chopped

2 tablespoons oil

4 oz. breadcrumbs

grated rind of 1 lemon

1½ teaspoons marjoram

6 oz. mushrooms, finely chopped

1 egg, beaten

1 oz. butter

½ beef stock cube, dissolved in ¼ pint water

2 teaspoons flour

2 teaspoons tomato purée

1 – 2 tablespoons water

finely chopped parsley

Beat and flatten beef slices with a wet rolling pin until very thin. Season. Cook onion gently in 1 tablespoon of the oil for about 5 minutes, until soft. In a bowl mix thoroughly breadcrumbs, onion, lemon rind, marjoram, mushrooms and season. Add beaten egg to bind. Divide mixture equally between beef slices. Roll up neatly and tie securely with thin string. Heat butter and remaining oil in a frying pan, add beef olives and brown on all sides. Pour in stock and bring to the boil. Transfer to a 3 pint ovenproof casserole. Cover and bake at 350 deg. F., Gas No. 4, for 1 hour 40 minutes, until tender. Remove string from beef olives, place on oval serving dish and keep warm. Blend flour with a little water, stir in tomato purée, blend in cooking stock and cook for 2 – 3 minutes, until sauce thickens. Check seasoning. Pour over beef olives. Garnish with chopped parsley.

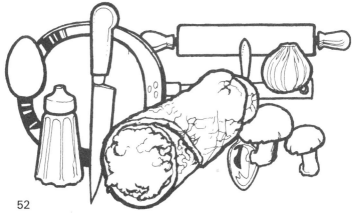

Beef Italian-style

Serves 4

Oven temperature 325 deg. F., Gas No. 3

1 lb. 4 oz. chuck steak, cut into $\frac{1}{2}$ inch cubes	2 teaspoons Italian seasoning
1 oz. seasoned flour	1 oz. raisins
1 tablespoon oil	1 eating apple
1 oz. butter	salt
2 medium onions, chopped	pepper
1 beef stock cube, dissolved in $\frac{3}{4}$ pint water	

Toss steak in seasoned flour. Heat oil and butter, add steak and brown on all sides. Place in a $2\frac{1}{2} - 3$ pint ovenproof casserole. Cook onion gently in remaining oil and butter for about $3 - 4$ minutes until soft. Add any remaining flour then gradually stir in stock, bring to the boil and cook for $2 - 3$ minutes. Pour over steak, add Italian seasoning and raisins. Core apple, cut into $\frac{1}{2}$ inch pieces and add to meat. Cover and bake at 325 deg. F., Gas No. 3, for $2 - 2\frac{1}{2}$ hours until tender. Check seasoning.

Serve with buttered pasta.

County Steak

Serves 4

Oven temperature 325 deg. F., Gas No. 3

1 lb. 8 oz. chuck steak	1 whole bay leaf
$\frac{1}{2}$ teaspoon meat tenderiser	$\frac{1}{2}$ teaspoon parsley
$1\frac{1}{2}$ oz. lard	salt
4 whole cloves	pepper
2 onions, peeled	1 pint water
$\frac{1}{2}$ teaspoon celery flakes	*Sauce*
6 black peppercorns	1 oz. flour
grated rind of $\frac{1}{2}$ lemon	$\frac{1}{4}$ pint port wine
pinch cayenne	1 tablespoon redcurrant
pinch ground mace	jelly

Cut steak in pieces, put on a plate. Sprinkle with meat tenderiser, pierce with a fork and leave 5 minutes. Melt lard in a pan, add meat and fry quickly until brown. Transfer to a $2\frac{1}{2}$ pint ovenproof casserole. Insert cloves in onions, add to casserole with celery, peppercorns, lemon rind, cayenne, mace and herbs. Add seasoning and water. Cover and bake at 325 deg. F., Gas No. 3, for 2½ hours or until tender. Sieve gravy into a pan. Keep meat hot in serving dish. Blend flour to smooth paste in a bowl with a little gravy. Add to gravy in pan. Simmer until thick then add port and redcurrant jelly and simmer until dissolved. Adjust seasoning, pour gravy over meat.

Celebration Beef

Serves 6

Oven temperature 450 deg. F., Gas No. 8

1 fillet of beef, about 2 lb 8 oz.	2 oz. mushrooms, finely chopped
1 oz. lard	salt
2 teaspoons instant minced onion	pepper
2 teaspoons water	13½ oz. packet frozen puff pastry, thawed
8 teaspoons Dijon mustard	1 egg, beaten
2 teaspoons bouquet garni for beef	
2 teaspoons mushroom powder	

Trim fillet to make a compact shape. Place in a roasting pan, spread with lard and bake at 450 deg. F., Gas No. 8, for 10 minutes to seal. Remove and cool. Meanwhile soak onion in water for 15 minutes. Stir in mustard, bouquet garni for beef, mushroom powder, mushrooms, salt and pepper.

Roll out pastry very thinly to an oblong large enough to completely enclose the fillet and allowing for a good overlap when sealing. Trim off edges. Spread pastry with mushroom mixture to within 2 inches of edges. Place fillet in centre of pastry, brush edges with beaten egg and wrap up like a parcel, making sure all edges are sealed. Place in a baking pan, sealed side down. Cut leaves from pastry trimmings and use to decorate top. Chill. Brush with beaten egg and bake at 450 deg. F., Gas No. 8, for 35 – 40 minutes until pastry is browned.

Spiced Beef with Garlic and Herb Sauce

Serves 4 – 6

2 lb. topside of beef	*Sauce*
$\frac{3}{4}$ pint water	1 carton soured cream
$\frac{1}{4}$ pint vinegar	$\frac{1}{4}$ teaspoon instant
2 teaspoons pickling spice	minced garlic
1 onion	$\frac{1}{2}$ teaspoon mixed fine herbs
1 tablespoon oil	$\frac{1}{2}$ oz. flour
$\frac{1}{4}$ pint water	

Place beef in a bowl together with $\frac{3}{4}$ pint water, vinegar and pickling spice and soak overnight, turning occasionally. Cut onion into wedges and cook gently in oil in a large saucepan for 2–3 minutes. Drain beef thoroughly and place in saucepan with onion. Seal on all sides. Add $\frac{1}{4}$ pint water and simmer gently for 40 minutes to 1 hour according to preference i.e. 40 minutes for rare beef, 50 minutes for medium rare, 1 hour for well done. While beef is cooking stir minced garlic and fine herbs into soured cream. When beef is cooked, remove and keep hot on serving dish. Strain cooking liquor. Blend flour with $\frac{1}{4}$ pint of cooking liquor and bring to the boil, stirring. Remove from heat and stir in soured cream. Reheat but do not boil.

Spiced Beef Pie

Serves 4

Oven temperature 375 deg. F., Gas No. 5

1 lb. minced beef, cooked or raw	salt
	pepper
1 onion, finely chopped	8 oz. cooked potatoes, sliced
2 tablespoons tomato purée	1 oz. Cheddar cheese, grated
1 teaspoon bouquet garni for beef	$\frac{1}{2}$ oz. butter
1 teaspoon ground nutmeg	

If using raw minced meat, cook in frying pan with onion until brown. Pour off excess fat. If cooked mince is used, soften onion in $\frac{1}{2}$ oz. dripping. Heat together in pan mince, onion, tomato purée, spices and season to taste. Turn into 2 pint ovenproof dish. Cover top with overlapping slices of potato, sprinkle with cheese and dot with butter. Bake at 375 deg. F., Gas No. 5, for 25 – 30 minutes, until cheese is golden and potatoes are crisp.

Chilli Con Carne

Serves 4

2 oz. butter
1 large onion, finely chopped
1 green pepper, finely chopped
1 lb. raw minced beef
½ teaspoon chilli seasoning

15 oz. can red kidney beans, drained
½ teaspoon salt
2 tablespoons tomato purée
¼ pint water or stock

Melt butter in a saucepan. Add onion and green pepper and cook gently for 3 – 4 minutes, until just soft. Add mince and brown, stirring with a fork to prevent it sticking. Add all other ingredients. Bring to the boil and simmer very gently for 35 minutes. Stir halfway through the cooking adding a little water if necessary.

Spaghetti Bolognese

Serves 4

1 large onion, chopped
1 tablespoon oil
1 lb. raw minced beef
14 oz. can tomatoes
1 beef stock cube
2 teaspoons tomato purée

2 teaspoons bouquet garni for beef
salt
pepper
12 oz. spaghetti
½ oz. butter
1 oz. Parmesan cheese

Add onion to heated oil in a saucepan. Cook gently for 2 – 3 minutes without colouring. Add minced beef and brown evenly, stirring continuously with a fork, to separate the pieces. Add tomatoes with juice from can, crumbled stock cube, tomato purée bouquet garni for beef, salt and pepper. Bring to the boil, then simmer gently for 30 minutes. Check seasoning. Cook spaghetti in boiling salted water for 15 – 20 minutes until just tender. Drain thoroughly and toss in butter. To serve, arrange spaghetti as a border on a large round plate. Pour bolognese sauce into the centre and sprinkle with Parmesan cheese. Serve with extra cheese as accompaniment.

Green Peppers Italienne

Serves 4

Oven temperature 350 deg. F., Gas No. 4

1 large onion, finely chopped	2 teaspoons Italian seasoning
2 tablespoons oil	salt
1 lb. raw minced beef	pepper
2 tablespoons tomato purée	4 green peppers
4 oz. mushrooms, sliced	

Cook onion gently in oil for 2 – 3 minutes. Add minced beef and fry, stirring until browned. Add tomato purée, mushrooms, Italian seasoning, salt and pepper and cook for 5 minutes. Blanch peppers in boiling salted water. Cut a slice off stalk ends and remove seeds. Fill pepper with beef mixture and replace top slice. Place in large buttered ovenproof dish, cover with foil and bake at 350 deg. F., Gas No. 4, for 45 minutes.

Lamb Provençale

Serves 4

Oven temperature 425 deg. F., Gas No. 7

1 lb. 8 oz. boned middle neck of lamb	1 chicken stock cube, dissolved in $\frac{3}{4}$ pint water
$\frac{1}{2}$ oz. flour	
2 large onions, sliced into rings	$\frac{1}{8}$ teaspoon garlic powder
14 oz. can tomatoes	1 tablespoon bouquet garni for lamb
1 lb. potatoes, peeled and thinly sliced	$\frac{1}{2}$ oz. butter, melted

Cut meat into equal-sized pieces and toss in flour. Place a layer of onions on bottom of a 4 pint ovenproof casserole, add half of the meat on top, followed by half the tomatoes and top with a thin layer of sliced potatoes. Repeat these layers once more arranging potatoes neatly overlapping on top. Mix stock with garlic powder and bouquet garni and pour over the casserole. Cover and bake at 425 deg. F., Gas No. 7, for 20 minutes. Reduce to 350 deg. F., Gas No. 4, for a further 1 hour 40 minutes. 30 minutes before the end of cooking time, brush butter on potato, continue cooking without lid and allow topping to brown.

Lamb Stew with Small Dumplings
Serves 4

1 lb. 8 oz. lamb, taken from a 2 lb. 4 oz. piece of shoulder

1 oz. butter

3 medium carrots, peeled and sliced

2 medium onions, peeled and sliced

3 sticks celery, sliced

pepper

1 teaspoon rosemary

1 chicken stock cube, dissolved in $\frac{3}{4}$ pint water

Breadcrumb Dumplings

8 oz. breadcrumbs, soaked in 4 tablespoons of milk

2 oz. butter

1 egg

$\frac{1}{2}$ teaspoon salt

pepper

Trim off excess fat from meat and cut in $\frac{1}{2}$ inch cubes. Heat butter in a large saucepan, add lamb and seal quickly on all sides without browning. Add carrots, onions, celery, pepper and rosemary. Pour over stock, cover with lid and simmer very gently for $1\frac{1}{2}$ hours until meat is tender. Check seasoning before adding dumplings.

Prepare dumplings about 30 minutes before the lamb is cooked. Soak breadcrumbs in milk. Cream butter, beat in egg and breadcrumbs. Add salt and pepper. Form into 8 small balls. Plunge dumplings into boiling salted water and cook for 5 minutes. Drain and add to lamb for the last 10 minutes of cooking time, so that they absorb flavour from the stock.

Baby Lamb en Croûte
Serves 4

Oven temperature 425 deg. F., Gas No. 7

8 lean baby lamb cutlets

salt

pepper

2 oz. butter

$\frac{1}{2}$ teaspoon garlic powder

$\frac{1}{2}$ teaspoon rosemary

11 oz. pack frozen puff pastry, thawed

1 egg, beaten with 1 tablespoon water

Trim off any excess fat from cutlets, season both sides with salt and pepper. Soften butter, add garlic and rosemary. Use to spread one side of each cutlet. Roll out pastry to an oblong about 11" x 21". Using a sharp knife cut out 8 rounds, using a 5 inch saucer as a guide. Place a cutlet on each round of pastry and damp edges with beaten egg. Fold over so that the end of the rib bone sticks out. Seal firmly at the side. Place on a baking tray and brush with beaten egg. Bake at 425 deg. F., Gas No. 7, for 25 – 30 minutes until golden brown. Remove and arrange on oval serving plate. Decorate the bones with cutlet frills. Serve with tossed green salad.

Scotch Mutton Pies

Serves 4

Oven temperature 425 deg. F., Gas No. 7

1 lb. raw mutton, minced	*Shortcrust pastry*
$\frac{1}{2}$ oz. dripping	1 lb. plain flour
6 oz. can condensed creamed vegetable soup	1 teaspoon salt
	6 oz. lard
2 teaspoons mushroom powder	6 oz. butter
2 teaspoons instant minced onion	about 5 tablespoons cold water
salt	1 egg, blended with 1 tablespoon water
pepper	

Fry meat in dripping about 5 minutes or until lightly browned, stirring. Stir in remaining ingredients and simmer, uncovered, for 45 minutes until meat is tender. Drain off excess fat. Check seasoning and leave until cold.

To make shortcrust pastry rub fats into flour and salt until mixture resembles fine breadcrumbs. Mix to a stiff dough with water. Knead lightly and roll out thinly. Cut 8 ovals, each about 5" × 3", using a plain cutter. Cut eight slightly larger ovals with remaining pastry. Divide cold meat mixture between eight small ovals. Dampen edges of pastry with blended egg and water and cover with larger ovals. Seal edges and make a pattern round edges with a fork. Decorate each with a pastry leaf made from trimmings. Place on a baking tray. Brush tops of pies with blended egg and bake at 425 deg. F., Gas No. 7, about 25 minutes or until golden brown.

Oriental Lamb Casserole

Serves 4

Oven temperature 350 deg. F., Gas No. 4

1 best end of neck of lamb, about 2 lb.

1 oz. butter

2 medium onions, chopped

1 tablespoon tomato purée

1 teaspoon ground ginger

$\frac{1}{2}$ teaspoon ground nutmeg

$\frac{1}{2}$ teaspoon ground cumin seed

1 chicken stock cube, dissolved in $\frac{1}{2}$ pint water

1 oz. raisins

2 teaspoons salt

pepper

$\frac{1}{2}$ oz. cornflour

Cut neck of lamb into joints. Melt butter in a heavy saucepan and fry meat until brown on both sides. Remove from pan and pour off most of the fat. Add onion and cook gently until soft. Stir in tomato purée and spices and cook for 1 minute. Add stock, raisins, seasoning and lamb. Cover and simmer gently for 45 – 60 minutes or transfer to a 3 pint ovenproof casserole and bake at 350 deg. F., Gas No. 4, for 1 – 1$\frac{1}{4}$ hours. Just before serving skim off any excess fat from top. Mix cornflour with a little cold water and blend into casserole. Cook another 5 minutes to thicken the sauce. Check seasoning.

Serve with plain boiled rice.

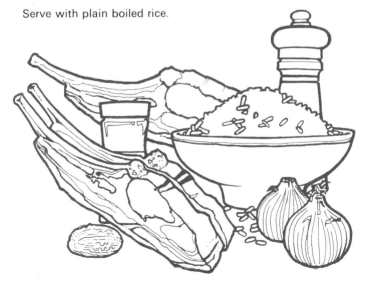

Marinated Lamb with Rice

Serves 4

Oven temperature 350 deg. F., Gas No. 4

1 lb. 8 oz. leg of lamb

2 × 5 oz. cartons natural yogurt

1 tablespoon onion flakes

$\frac{1}{2}$ teaspoon ground ginger

$\frac{1}{2}$ teaspoon chilli seasoning

1 teaspoon ground cumin seed

$\frac{1}{4}$ teaspoon turmeric

$\frac{1}{4}$ teaspoon ground allspice

$\frac{1}{2}$ teaspoon garlic salt

$\frac{1}{4}$ teaspoon ground black pepper

1 teaspoon lemon juice

$\frac{1}{2}$ teaspoon salt

Rice

1 pint water

1 teaspoon salt

6 oz. long grain rice

$\frac{1}{4}$ teaspoon turmeric

8 whole cloves

6 whole bay leaves

12 black peppercorns

$\frac{1}{2}$ teaspoon cinnamon

1 tomato, sliced for garnish

Trim off fat from lamb and cut into 1 inch cubes. In a 3 pint oven-proof casserole mix together yogurt, onion flakes, all the spices, lemon juice and salt. Stir in lamb and marinate for 4 hours, stirring occasionally. Cover and bake at 350 deg. F., Gas No. 4, for 1$\frac{1}{2}$ hours till lamb is tender.

For the rice bring water and salt to the boil. Add rice and remaining ingredients, except tomato, stir, cover tightly and simmer for 15 minutes till water is absorbed and rice cooked. Add a little extra water if required. Remove bay leaves and turn rice onto a large serving platter making a border. Pile lamb in the centre. Garnish with sliced tomato.

Barbecued Spare Ribs

Serves 6

Oven temperature 350 deg. F., Gas No. 4

4 lb. spare ribs of pork

boiling water

Marinade

4 tablespoons vinegar

2 tablespoons tomato purée

1 tablespoon soy sauce

$\frac{1}{2}$ teaspoon sweet basil

$\frac{1}{2}$ teaspoon garlic powder

$\frac{1}{4}$ teaspoon chilli seasoning

2 tablespoons brown sugar

salt

pepper

Cover spare ribs with boiling water and simmer for 40 minutes. Drain well.

Combine marinade ingredients in a saucepan and bring to boil. Pour over spare ribs and leave to marinate for a minimum of 4 hours at room temperature or overnight in a refrigerator.
Place spare ribs on barbecue rack or spit. Brush with marinade during cooking and turn over occasionally. Barbecue for 25 – 30 minutes. If cooking in an oven bake at 350 deg. F., Gas No. 4, for 50 minutes, basting occasionally. Heat up remaining marinade and serve with spare ribs.

Danish Meat Balls with Onion Sauce
Serves 6

12 oz. lean pork
12 oz. lean stewing beef
$\frac{1}{2}$ teaspoon meat tenderiser
6 oz. fresh white breadcrumbs
1 onion, finely chopped
$1\frac{1}{2}$ teaspoons salt
$\frac{1}{4}$ teaspoon ground black pepper
$\frac{1}{4}$ teaspoon ground mace
$\frac{1}{4}$ teaspoon ground bay leaves
2 tablespoons chopped parsley

1 egg, beaten
oil or fat for frying

Sauce
2 oz. dripping
4 onions, chopped
1 teaspoon caster sugar
$1\frac{1}{2}$ oz. flour
1 beef stock cube, dissolved in 1 pint water
2 teaspoons tomato purée
$\frac{1}{4}$ teaspoon chilli seasoning
salt
pepper

Cut meat in strips and sprinkle with meat tenderiser. Leave 5 minutes then mince finely. Mix with all ingredients except egg. Add sufficient egg to bind mixture together. Heat about 1 inch oil or fat in a pan. Dip a tablespoon in hot fat then gently drop rounded tablespoons of meat mixture into fat. Fry on medium heat for about 8 minutes, turning once. Drain on kitchen paper and keep hot. Meanwhile melt dripping for sauce in a pan. Fry onions slowly until soft and golden. Add sugar and cook for 3 minutes more. Blend in flour and cook 1 minute then add beef stock and bring to boiling point, stirring. Add remaining ingredients and simmer 10 minutes. Serve sauce with meat balls.

Fireside Skewers

Serves 4

12 oz. fillet or leg of lamb
1 tablespoon bouquet garni for lamb
1 tablespoon barbecue seasoning
salt
pepper
½ pint cider

1 large stick celery, cut into 8 pieces
1 dessert apple
8 oz. button mushrooms
oil or butter for brushing
½ oz. butter
½ oz. flour
few drops gravy browning

Trim meat, cut into 1 inch cubes and place in a deep dish. Sprinkle with bouquet garni, barbecue seasoning, salt and pepper. Pour over cider and marinate, covered, for 6 hours or overnight in the refrigerator. Turn occasionally. Drain and reserve marinade.

Blanch celery in boiling salted water for 5 minutes. Cut un-peeled apple into 8 pieces and remove core. Thread lamb, apple, mushrooms and celery onto 4 skewers. Brush well with oil or melted butter and place under a moderately hot grill for about 10 minutes, turning skewers several times.

Melt ½ oz. butter, add flour and cook for 1 minute. Remove from heat and gradually add marinade. Bring to the boil, stirring, until sauce thickens. Add gravy browning to give a rich colour and check seasoning.

Serve on plain boiled rice with food removed from skewers and sauce poured on top.

Barbecued Stuffed Pork Chops

Serves 4

Oven temperature 425 deg. F., Gas No. 7

4 large pork chops	$\frac{1}{4}$ teaspoon salt
Stuffing	pepper
1 oz. butter	
1 medium onion, finely chopped	1 tablespoon oil
4 oz. mushrooms, finely chopped	1 teaspoon barbecue seasoning
$\frac{1}{2}$ teaspoon ground mace	

Carefully remove the bones from the pork chops. In each make a horizontal cut, forming a 'pocket' within the chop.

Melt butter in saucepan, add onion and cook gently until soft. Add mushrooms and continue cooking for 2 – 3 minutes, stirring continuously. Add mace and season well. Allow to cool slightly, divide equally and use to stuff the 'pockets' of each chop. Brush chops with oil on both sides and sprinkle with barbecue seasoning. Place in a roasting pan and bake at 425 deg. F., Gas No. 7, for 20 – 25 minutes.

Hungarian Pork Casserole

Serves 4

Oven temperature 350 deg. F., Gas No. 4

2 medium onions, sliced	$\frac{1}{4}$ pint red wine
1 tablespoon oil	1 beef stock cube, dissolved in $\frac{1}{4}$ pint water
1 oz. butter	
1 lb. 4 oz. pork fillet	$\frac{1}{4}$ teaspoon garlic salt
1 oz. seasoned flour	14 oz. can tomatoes
1 tablespoon paprika	5 oz. carton soured cream

Cook onions gently in oil and butter in a frying pan for about 7 – 10 minutes. Cut meat into 1 inch cubes. Toss in seasoned flour. Add to onions, together with paprika and cook for about 2 – 3 minutes. Remove from heat and gradually stir in wine, stock, garlic salt and tomatoes with juice. Bring to boil for 2 – 3 minutes, until sauce thickens. Transfer to a 3 pint oven-proof casserole, cover and bake at 350 deg. F., Gas No. 4, for $1\frac{1}{2}$ hours until meat is tender. Check seasoning. Top with soured cream just before serving.

Barbecued Pork Fillet

Serves 4

1 lb. pork fillet, thinly sliced
½ oz. lard
1 large onion, chopped
½ teaspoon garlic salt
2¼ oz. can tomato purée
4 tablespoons water
2 tablespoons soft brown sugar

3 tablespoon vinegar
1 teaspoon Worcestershire sauce
¼ teaspoon steak spice
2 tablespoons mustard powder

Fry fillet slices quickly in lard until brown, turning once. Remove meat from pan. Add onion to pan and fry 5 minutes. Add all other ingredients, including meat. Cover and simmer 15 minutes. Serve with plain boiled rice.

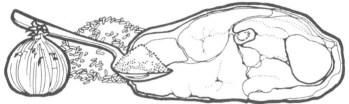

Veal Goulash

Serves 4

Oven temperature 350 deg. F., Gas No. 4

1 oz. butter
1 tablespoon oil
1 large onion
1 lb. 8 oz. stewing veal, cut into ½ inch cubes
2 tablespoons paprika

1 oz. seasoned flour
1 beef stock cube, dissolved in ¾ pint water
salt
pepper

Melt butter with oil in a frying pan and cook onion gently for about 5 minutes. Remove and keep on one side. Toss veal in paprika and seasoned flour. Fry meat to seal thoroughly on all sides. Stir in any remaining paprika and seasoned flour, cook for 2 minutes and remove from heat. Add onions, stock and bring to the boil for 2 – 3 minutes, stirring continuously. Transfer to a 3 pint ovenproof casserole, cover with lid and bake at 350 deg F., Gas No. 4, for 1½ hours, until meat is tender. Check seasoning. Serve with buttered noodles.

Veal Tansy

Serves 4

Oven temperature 350 deg. F., Gas No. 4

2 large carrots
1 tablespoon oil
1 oz. butter
2 large onions, quartered or 12 button onions
1 lb. 4 oz. stewing veal, cut into $\frac{1}{2}$ inch cubes
1 oz. seasoned flour
1 chicken stock cube, dissolved in $\frac{1}{2}$ pint water
8 oz. can tomatoes
$\frac{1}{4}$ teaspoon ground mace
1 tablespoon parsley
rind and juice of 1 lemon

Cut carrots into $\frac{1}{4}$ inch slices. Heat oil and butter in a large saucepan. Add vegetables, cover with a lid and cook gently without browning for 10 minutes. Toss veal in seasoned flour. Add to vegetables and cook until lightly coloured, stirring frequently. Add stock, tomatoes with juice, mace and parsley and bring to the boil. Turn down and simmer for 45 minutes or turn into a 3 pint ovenproof dish, cover and bake at 350 deg. F., Gas No. 4, for 45 – 50 minutes, until veal is tender. Add lemon juice and rind just before serving. Check seasoning.

Cidered Veal Paprika

Serves 4

1 lb. 4 oz. shoulder of veal
$\frac{1}{2}$ oz. seasoned flour
1 tablespoon oil
1 oz. butter
1 medium onion, chopped
2 tablespoons paprika
$\frac{1}{2}$ pint cider
1 chicken stock cube
$\frac{1}{2}$ oz. flour, blended with 2 tablespoons water
$\frac{1}{4}$ pint single cream
4 oz. green grapes

Trim veal, cut into long strips $\frac{1}{2}$ inch in thickness and toss in seasoned flour. Fry quickly in a saucepan in heated oil and butter to seal. Remove and keep on one side. Cook onion gently for 2 – 3 minutes in remaining oil until soft. Stir in paprika, cider and crumbled stock cube and bring to boil. Return veal to pan and simmer gently for 1 hour, until veal is tender. Stir in flour blended with water and bring to boil gently for 2 – 3 minutes. Remove from heat and stir in cream. Check seasoning. Turn into serving dish and garnish with halved and de-pipped grapes and serve with plain boiled rice.

Spiced Orange Gammon Parcels

Serves 4

Oven temperature 425 deg. F., Gas No. 7

4 thick gammon steaks whole cloves	2 oranges 1 teaspoon ground cinnamon

Trim off any excess fat from gammon. Place each steak on individual large pieces of foil on a baking tray. Squeeze juice from oranges and mix with cinnamon. Place 4 whole cloves on each gammon steak and pour over orange juice. Seal foil loosely and bake at 425 deg. F., Gas No. 7, for 25 – 30 minutes.

Gammon with White Peaches

Serves 4 – 6

Oven temperature 350 deg. F., Gas No. 4

2 lb. gammon joint, pre-soaked for 24 hours whole cloves	juice of 1 lemon $\frac{1}{2}$ teaspoon mustard powder 1 teaspoon ground cinnamon
Glaze	$\frac{1}{4}$ teaspoon whole cloves
$\frac{1}{4}$ pint water 4 oz. soft brown sugar	15 oz. can white peaches, drained

Place gammon in pan of cold water. Bring to the boil and cook for 20 minutes. Remove from liquid and cool slightly. Remove skin from joint and slash fat neatly into $\frac{1}{2}$ inch diamonds. Stud the centre of each diamond with a whole clove. Place in a baking pan.

Place water and sugar in a saucepan, heat gently until sugar dissolves. Add lemon juice, mustard, cinnamon and whole cloves. Cook rapidly and reduce glaze by half. Strain over gammon and cover with foil. Bake at 350 deg. F., Gas No. 4, for $1\frac{1}{2}$ hours, basting occasionally. Half an hour before the end of cooking time, remove foil, baste the joint and add the drained peaches. Continue cooking so that the fat crisps and turns golden brown.

Glazed Gammon with Grapefruit

Serves 4

Oven temperature 350 deg. F., Gas No. 4

3 lb. joint of gammon, pre-soaked if necessary

$\frac{1}{4}$ pint unsweetened grapefruit juice, or juice of 1 grapefruit

2 oz. soft brown sugar

$\frac{1}{2}$ teaspoon mixed spice

1 grapefruit

1 tablespoon made mustard

glacé cherries

whole cloves

Simmer gammon in water for 1 hour. Reserve $\frac{1}{4}$ pint of stock for sauce. Remove skin from gammon. Bring grapefruit juice, brown sugar and mixed spice to the boil and reduce to half the quantity.

Meanwhile remove skin and pith from grapefruit. Cut grapefruit into round slices. Place gammon in a baking pan and spread fat with mustard.

Secure grapefruit slices onto the ham fat with cocktail sticks, placing half a cherry in centre of each slice. Stud with cloves between slices. Pour over grapefruit glaze and bake at 350 deg. F., Gas No. 4, for about 1 hour, basting frequently with glaze. When cooked remove joint and place on serving dish.

Add $\frac{1}{4}$ pint of ham stock to remaining glaze in pan, bring to the boil and simmer for two minutes. Serve as a sauce with the gammon.

Braised Kidneys with Basil

Serves 4

Oven temperature 375 deg. F., Gas No. 5

1 lb. lamb's or pig's kidneys
1 medium onion, chopped
1 oz. butter
8 oz. mushrooms

$10\frac{1}{2}$ oz. can condensed tomato soup
$\frac{1}{2}$ soup can water
3 teaspoons sweet basil

Remove skin, cut kidneys in half and remove cores. If using kidneys, cut in slices. Place in a $2\frac{1}{2}$ pint ovenproof dish. Cook onion gently in butter for 2–3 minutes without browning. Wash mushrooms and cut into quarters. Add to onion. Stir in condensed soup, water and sweet basil, bring to the boil and pour over kidneys. Cover dish with foil and bake at 375 deg. F., Gas No. 5, for 45 minutes. Serve with plain boiled rice.

Veal and Ham Galantine

Serves 4

1 teaspoon powdered gelatine
1 tablespoon water
15 oz. can consommé
8 oz. cooked veal, finely diced

4 oz. ham, finely diced
2 teaspoons mixed fine herbs
$\frac{1}{2}$ teaspoon salt
$\frac{1}{8}$ teaspoon pepper
2 hard-boiled eggs, sliced
sprigs of parsley

Dissolve gelatine with water in bowl over a pan of hot water. Add consommé and heat until melted. Pour a thin layer of consommé into a 2 pint mould or loaf tin, leave in refrigerator until set. Add all other ingredients except egg and parsley to remaining consommé. Mix well and check seasoning. Cover base of mould with overlapping egg slices. Spoon in meat mixture, leave in refrigerator several hours until set. Turn out onto a flat serving dish and garnish with parsley sprigs.

Poultry & Game

Grilled Chicken with Lemon and Herbs
Serves 4

4 roasting chicken joints	1 teaspoon mixed fine herbs
salt	grated rind and juice of
pepper	$\frac{1}{2}$ lemon
2 oz. butter	4 lemon wedges

Sprinkle chicken joints with salt and pepper.

Beat butter to soften and add fine herbs, lemon rind and juice. Spread butter mixture over chicken joints. Place on foil on grill pan and cook under a moderately hot grill for 20 – 25 minutes, turning about 3 times and basting with butter. Serve with lemon wedges.

Roast Chicken with Rice and Apricot Stuffing
Serves 4

Oven temperature 375 deg. F., Gas No. 5

1 oz. butter	3 lb. roasting chicken
1 small onion, finely chopped	2 oz. butter
3 stalks celery, finely chopped	8 oz. can apricot halves
8 oz. cooked long grain rice (3 oz. uncooked)	2 teaspoons cornflour
3 oz. dried apricots, chopped	$\frac{1}{4}$ pint chicken stock, made from giblets
1 teaspoon marjoram	2 teaspoons vinegar (optional)
$\frac{1}{2}$ teaspoon ground oregano	
1 teaspoon thyme	
salt	
pepper	

Melt butter in a frying pan and cook onion and celery gently until soft. Remove from heat and stir in rice, dried apricots and herbs. Season to taste. Wash and dry chicken. Stuff cavity with rice mixture and truss with string or a skewer. Rub breast with 2 oz. butter, season well and cover breast with foil. Place in a roasting pan and cook in oven at 375 deg. F., Gas No. 5, for 1 – 1¼ hours, basting frequently. Remove foil 15 minutes before end of cooking time.

Drain apricots, reserving juice. Place chicken on hot serving dish, arrange apricot halves around dish and keep hot. Pour off fat in pan, reserving about 2 tablespoons. Mix cornflour with a little apricot juice and stir into fat together with remaining juice and chicken stock. Bring to the boil, stirring until thickened. Check seasoning. If sauce is too sweet stir in 1 – 2 teaspoons of vinegar.

Chicken and Onion Casserole

Serves 4

Oven temperature 375 deg. F., Gas No. 5

1 teaspoon oil	2 teaspoons poultry
4 roasting chicken joints	seasoning
1½ pint packet white onion soup	salt
	pepper
14 oz. can tomatoes	

Heat oil in a large frying pan. Add chicken and brown evenly. Remove to a 4 pint ovenproof casserole. Place onion soup in a measuring jug and make up to ½ pint with cold water, and mix well. Pour into frying pan, add tomatoes and juice and bring to the boil for 2 – 3 minutes, stirring continuously. Add poultry seasoning and additional seasoning if required. Pour over chicken portions, cover with lid or foil and bake at 375 deg. F., Gas No. 5, for 1½ hours, until chicken is tender.

Chicken with Tarragon and Lemon

Serves 4

Oven temperature 350 deg. F., Gas No. 4

4 roasting chicken joints	2 egg yolks
1 oz. seasoned flour	2 tablespoons single cream
1 oz. butter	salt
1 tablespoon oil	pepper
rind and juice of 1 lemon	slices of lemon
1 tablespoon tarragon leaves	
½ chicken stock cube, dissolved in ½ pint water	

Toss chicken joints in seasoned flour. Heat butter and oil in large frying pan. Add chicken and brown well on all sides. Place in a 4 pint ovenproof casserole. Mix lemon rind, tarragon and stock and bring to the boil. Pour over chicken. Cover and bake at 350 deg. F., Gas No. 4, for 1¼ – 1½ hours, until chicken is tender. Remove chicken, place on serving dish and keep hot. Pour stock into a small pan. Blend egg yolks with cream and add a little of the chicken stock. Return to the pan together with lemon juice and reheat but do not boil. Check seasoning. Pour over chicken and garnish with twists of lemon.

Paprika Spiced Chicken
Serves 4

4 roasting chicken joints
1 teaspoon instant minced onion
$\frac{1}{4}$ teaspoon ground mace
6 black peppercorns
$\frac{1}{4}$ teaspoon thyme
rind of 1 lemon
$\frac{1}{2}$ teaspoon parsley
1 teaspoon salt
$1\frac{1}{2}$ pints water

Sauce
2 oz. butter
2 oz. flour
1 tablespoon paprika
$\frac{1}{2}$ teaspoon made mustard
2 tablespoons redcurrant jelly
salt
pepper
5 oz. carton soured cream
1 canned red pepper, cut into strips

Put chicken joints in a large pan. Add all other ingredients and bring to boiling point. Cover and simmer for 30 minutes or until joints are tender. Remove joints from pan, place on a serving dish and keep hot. Strain cooking liquor into a measuring jug and make up to 1 pint with water if necessary.

Melt butter for sauce in a pan, blend in flour and cook 1 minute. Add paprika and cook a further minute. Stir in mustard and stock. Bring to boiling point, stirring. Simmer 2 minutes then add redcurrant jelly and simmer until dissolved. Add seasoning. Remove from heat and add soured cream. Pour sauce over chicken joints. Garnish with narrow strips of pepper.

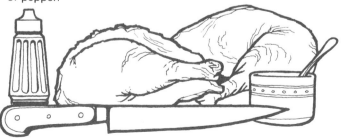

Summer Chicken Pie

Serves 6

Oven temperature 375 deg. F., Gas No. 5

Pastry

6 oz. plain flour
½ teaspoon salt
3 oz. butter
2 tablespoons water

Filling

1 oz. butter
1 onion, finely chopped
12 oz. cooked chicken meat, roughly chopped

2 teaspoons mushroom powder
4 oz. liver sausage, skinned and cut into ½ inch cubes
¼ pint single cream
¾ teaspoon chervil
¼ teaspoon oregano
salt
pepper
milk for glazing

Mix together flour and salt. Rub in butter until mixture resembles fine breadcrumbs. Mix to a stiff dough with water. Knead lightly and allow to rest in a cool place for 30 minutes. Melt butter in a small pan and cook onion gently until soft, about 5 minutes. Place chicken pieces, mushroom powder, liver sausage and onion in a bowl. Blend together cream, herbs and seasoning, pour over chicken and mix thoroughly. Turn onto a well-buttered 8 inch pie plate.

Roll out pastry to a circle and cover pie in the usual way. Decorate top with pastry leaves cut from trimmings. Brush with milk and bake at 375 deg. F., Gas No. 5, for 30 minutes until pastry is golden. Leave to cool.

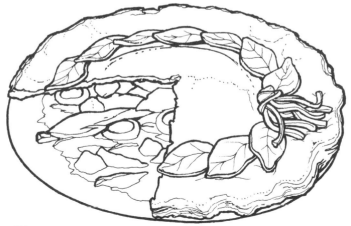

Chicken and Red Pepper Salad
Serves 4

Dressing
1 teaspoon caster sugar
1 teaspoon salt
1 teaspoon made mustard
pepper
$\frac{1}{2}$ teaspoon chervil
1 tablespoon celery flakes
4 tablespoons salad oil
1 tablespoon wine vinegar

12 oz. cooked chicken meat
1 oz. butter
1 onion, finely chopped
4 oz. long grain rice
1 chicken stock cube, dissolved in $\frac{3}{4}$ pint water
3 oz. can red peppers, drained and chopped
4 oz. button mushrooms, thinly sliced
1 oz. flaked almonds, toasted

Blend together all ingredients for dressing and leave for at least 2 hours. Cut chicken meat into small pieces. Melt butter and fry onion gently for 2 – 3 minutes. Add rice and fry, stirring, for 1 minute. Pour in stock and cook, uncovered, for 10 minutes, add peppers and mushrooms and continue cooking for about 5 minutes until rice is just cooked and all stock is absorbed. Add chicken, turn into a bowl and leave to cool. Pour dressing onto rice mixture and mix thoroughly. Turn into serving dish and scatter almonds on top.

Chicken Milan
Serves 4
Oven temperature 350 deg. F., Gas No. 4

4 roasting chicken joints
salt
pepper

Tomato Sauce
8 oz. can tomatoes
$\frac{1}{2}$ oz. cornflour
1 teaspoon chilli seasoning
1$\frac{1}{2}$ teaspoons poultry seasoning
2 teaspoons tomato purée

$\frac{1}{4}$ teaspoon salt

Cheese Topping
1 oz. butter
1 oz. flour
$\frac{1}{4}$ pint milk
4 tablespoons single cream
3 oz. Cheddar cheese, grated
salt
pepper
sprigs of parsley

Skin chicken and season with salt and pepper and place in a baking pan. Sieve tomatoes, blend with cornflour. Add chilli seasoning, poultry seasoning, tomato purée and salt. Place in a saucepan, bring to the boil for 2 – 3 minutes, stirring. Cover each chicken joint completely with the tomato sauce. Bake at 350 deg. F., Gas No. 4, for 1 hour until tender. Baste with tomato sauce halfway through cooking time.

Meanwhile prepare cheese topping. Melt butter, add flour and cook for 2 – 3 minutes. Remove from heat and gradually stir in milk, then cream. Bring to the boil and cook for 2 minutes, stirring. Add 2 oz. grated cheese, salt and pepper to taste. Cook for 1 minute but do not boil. Remove from heat and cover surface with wet greaseproof paper or polythene to prevent skin forming. Place cooked chicken joints in grill pan. Reheat cheese topping without boiling and carefully coat top of chicken. Sprinkle with remaining grated cheese and place under a hot grill until golden brown. Place on serving dish and garnish with sprigs of parsley.

Chicken Country-style
Serves 4
Oven temperature 350 deg. F., Gas No. 4

1 oz. butter	10 oz. can potatoes, drained
4 roasting chicken joints	1 large leek, sliced
1½ pint packet minestrone soup	2 teaspoons poultry seasoning
½ pint water	¼ teaspoon mixed fine herbs
8 oz. can tomatoes	

Melt butter in a frying pan, add chicken joints and brown on all sides. Place in a 4 pint ovenproof casserole. Blend soup with water, pour into frying pan, add remaining ingredients and bring to the boil, stirring.
Pour over chicken, cover and bake at 350 deg. F., Gas No. 4, for 1 – 1¼ hours until chicken is tender. Check seasoning.

Tandoori Chicken

Serves 4

Oven temperature 350 deg. F., Gas No. 4

4 roasting chicken joints

Marinade

2 cartons natural yogurt
½ teaspoon ground ginger
1 tablespoon paprika
½ teaspoon garlic powder
4 whole bay leaves

6 black peppercorns
1 tablespoon tomato purée
grated rind of 1 lemon
1 teaspoon salt

Garnish

sprigs of parsley
cucumber slices
lemon wedges

Wash and skin chicken. Prick well with a fork or skewer. Place in deep bowl or dish.

Place yogurt in bowl, add all other ingredients and mix well. Pour over chicken making sure that the quarters are all completely covered with marinade. Cover tightly with foil and leave in a cool place for 24 hours. At the end of this time remove bay leaves.

Place chicken on wire rack in a roasting pan. (Alternatively, the chicken may be skewered with long skewers, with the ends resting on sides of pan.) Coat each joint with any remaining marinade. Bake at 350 deg. F., Gas No. 4, for 1½ hours. Continue basting until all the marinade has been used. Serve on an oval dish garnished with sprigs of parsley, cucumber slices, lemon wedges and serve with cucumber and yogurt salad and boiled rice.

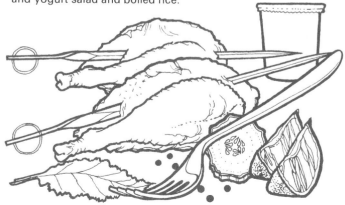

Madras Curry Powder

Makes about 3 oz.

1 oz. coriander seed

2 teaspoons garlic powder

1 tablespoon ground cumin seed

1 teaspoon ground ginger

1 teaspoon chilli seasoning

½ teaspoon ground allspice

2 teaspoons turmeric

1 tablespoon salt

1 tablespoon ground black pepper

½ tablespoon mustard powder

Grind coriander seed in an electric blender or with a pestle and mortar. Sieve to remove any large husks. Mix all ingredients together. Keep in an air-tight jar.

Chicken Madras

Serves 4

2 large onions, chopped

1 tablespoon oil

3 tablespoons Madras curry powder (see recipe above)

4 roasting chicken joints

2 teaspoons tomato purée

½ pint water

Cook onions gently in oil in large saucepan for 3–4 minutes. Add curry powder and continue to fry for 5 minutes, stirring continuously. Add chicken portions and continue frying for 10 minutes. Add tomato purée and water, bring to the boil, cover and simmer gently for about 1 hour. Serve with boiled rice, fried rice, onion salad, mango chutney and chapattis.

Normandy Duck

Serves 3 – 4

Oven temperature 425 deg. F., Gas No. 7

4 lb. roasting duck	pepper
1 oz. butter	2 dessert apples, peeled, cored and sliced
1 onion, chopped	
1 oz. flour	2 – 3 tablespoons cream
$\frac{1}{4}$ pint duck stock, made from giblets	*Garnish*
$\frac{1}{4}$ pint dry cider	1 red skinned dessert apple, unpeeled and sliced
1 teaspoon savory	juice of $\frac{1}{2}$ lemon
1 teaspoon marjoram	sprigs of parsley
salt	

Wash and dry duck and place in a roasting pan. Cook onion gently in butter until soft. Add flour and allow to brown then blend in stock and cider. Add herbs, seasoning and sliced apples. Pour over duck, cover with foil and bake at 425 deg. F., Gas No. 7, for 45 minutes. Remove foil and bake for a further 15 minutes until duck is tender. Remove duck and carve. Place meat on serving dish and keep warm. Remove any excess fat from sauce, stir in cream and reheat, but do not boil. Check seasoning. Spoon sauce around duck. Garnish with apple slices, brushed with lemon, and parsley sprigs.

Pheasant Casserole with Chestnuts

Serves 6

Oven temperature 325 deg. F., Gas No. 3

12 oz. chestnuts
1 large, pheasant, jointed
3 tablespoons oil
1 oz. butter
1 oz. flour
$\frac{1}{2}$ pint red wine
1 chicken stock cube, dissolved in $\frac{1}{2}$ pint water
8 oz. onions, cut in wedges

thinly peeled rind and juice of 1 orange
1 teaspoon redcurrant jelly
$\frac{1}{2}$ teaspoon salt
1 teaspoon bouquet garni for lamb
$\frac{1}{8}$ teaspoon ground black pepper
sprigs of parsley

Simmer chestnuts in boiling water about 2 minutes, drain, make a slit in each with a sharp knife. Remove outer skin. Simmer 20 minutes in water, then drain. Heat 2 tablespoons of oil in pan, add butter, fry pheasant until browned, turning once. Transfer joints to a 4 pint ovenproof casserole. Add remaining oil to pan with chestnuts, fry until evenly browned, drain on kitchen paper. Add flour to fat remaining in pan, cook gently until brown. Stir in wine and stock and bring to boiling point. Pour sauce into casserole, add all other ingredients except chestnuts and parsley. Cover and bake at 325 deg. F., Gas No. 3, for about $1\frac{1}{2} - 2$ hours until tender. Add chestnuts about 45 minutes before end of cooking time. Remove orange rind, check seasoning. Garnish with parsley sprigs before serving.

Young Jugged Hare

Serves 6

Oven temperature 325 deg. F., Gas No. 3

1 young hare
2 large onions, stuck
with 2 whole cloves each
½ teaspoon celery flakes
6 black peppercorns
rind of ½ lemon
pinch cayenne
¼ teaspoon thyme
1 whole bay leaf
1 teaspoon parsley
½ pint red wine

2 oz. bacon fat or lard
1½ pints water
salt
pepper
1 oz. butter
4 oz. button mushrooms,
thinly sliced

Liaison
2½ oz. butter
2 oz. flour
1 tablespoon redcurrant jelly

Ask butcher to skin and joint hare, which should be well hung. Discard intestines, reserve blood and liver. Put joints in a large bowl with sliced liver, onions, celery flakes, peppercorns, lemon rind, cayenne and herbs. Add wine, cover and leave in cool place overnight, turning occasionally. Drain hare joints, reserving marinade.

Melt bacon fat in a pan, add joints and fry briskly until brown, turning once. Put joints in a 6 pint ovenproof casserole with marinade, water and seasoning. Cover and bake at 325 deg. F., Gas No. 3, for 2 hours or until hare is tender. Melt butter in a small pan, add mushrooms and fry 2 minutes. Put on one side. Remove hare joints from casserole, arrange on a serving dish and keep hot. Melt butter for liaison in a clean pan, blend in flour and cook 1 minute. Strain gravy into pan and bring to boiling point, stirring. Add redcurrant jelly and mushrooms and simmer until jelly has dissolved. Remove pan from heat. Add reserved blood. Reheat but do not boil sauce or it will curdle. Pour sauce over joints.

Vegetables & Salads

Tomato, Chicory and Grape Salad
Serves 4

6 firm tomatoes, skinned
2 large heads chicory
8 oz. large black or white grapes, halved and pipped

3 tablespoons French dressing, (see page 36)
1 small onion, finely chopped
$\frac{1}{4}$ teaspoon marjoram

Quarter tomatoes and discard pips. Cut both heads of chicory in 8 pieces lengthways. Mix with tomato and grapes. Mix remaining ingredients, check seasoning, and mix into salad.

Red Cabbage Salad
Serves 4 – 6

8 oz. red cabbage, finely shredded
2 dessert apples, cored and sliced
4 sticks celery, chopped

Dressing
1 teaspoon salt
$\frac{1}{4}$ teaspoon pepper
1 tablespoon caster sugar
2 teaspoons French mustard
2 teaspoons onion powder
8 tablespoons vegetable oil
3 tablespoons cider vinegar

Blend together dressing ingredients in large bowl. Add cabbage, apple and celery and mix well. Cover and marinate in refrigerator overnight.

Apple, Celery and Potato Salad
Serves 4 – 6

2 teaspoons instant minced onion
3 teaspoons lemon juice
1 lb. 3 oz. can new potatoes, drained
1 small head celery, chopped

2 dessert apples, cored and diced
$\frac{1}{4}$ pint thick mayonnaise
salt
pepper

Soak onion in lemon juice.
Slice potatoes into a bowl. Add celery and apple. Stir in onion and remaining ingredients. Cover and leave in cool place several hours before serving.

Piquant Coleslaw
Serves 4 – 6

1 lb. firm white cabbage
2 oz. caster sugar
1 oz. plain flour
½ oz. mustard powder
1 teaspoon onion salt
1 oz. butter
2 egg yolks

⅛ pint vinegar
⅛ pint single cream
1 large carrot, grated
½ oz. sultanas
½ oz. seedless raisins
pepper
salt

Shred cabbage finely, discarding thick stems. Mix together sugar, flour, mustard and onion salt in a bowl. Stand bowl over a pan of simmering water. Add butter, egg yolks and vinegar. Stir well until thick. Remove from heat and leave until cold. Blend in cream. Stir dressing into cabbage. Add carrot, sultanas and raisins. Seasons with pepper and salt if necessary.

Beetroot and Horseradish Salad
Serves 4

1 lb. 4 oz. cooked beetroot, peeled
2 oz. can anchovies, drained
3 tablespoons horseradish cream
1 small dessert apple, peeled, cored and diced

Dressing
½ teaspoon salt
¼ teaspoon ground black pepper
½ teaspoon caster sugar
¼ teaspoon mixed fine herbs
1 tablespoon salad oil
2 teaspoons vinegar

Grate beetroot coarsely. Chop half of anchovies. Mix with beetroot. Add horseradish cream and apple. Blend together ingredients for dressing. Add to beetroot mixture. Turn into a serving dish. Decorate with remaining anchovy fillets.

Creamed Corn and Chive Salad
Serves 4 – 6

2 tablespoons thick
mayonnaise

4 tablespoons double cream,
whipped

2 teaspoons chives

$\frac{1}{4}$ teaspoon salad seasoning

salt

pepper

11 oz. can sweetcorn
kernels, drained

4 oz. button mushrooms,
thinly sliced

$\frac{1}{2}$ small green pepper, sliced

Combine mayonnaise, cream, chives, salad seasoning, salt
and pepper in a bowl. Add sweetcorn and mushrooms and
mix well. Turn into serving dish and leave for 2 hours.
Decorate round edge of dish with slices of green pepper
before serving.

Buttered Round Lettuce
Serves 4

3 lettuces

salt

1 teaspoon instant
minced onion

1 oz. butter

freshly ground black pepper

Discard 2 or 3 outside leaves of each lettuce. Remove some of
stalk from inner leaves. Shred leaves coarsely. Put in pan with
$\frac{1}{2}$ inch boiling salted water and instant minced onion. Cover and
simmer 5 – 10 minutes or until barely tender. Drain in a colander.
Press out excess water. Return to pan. Toss in butter and
season with pepper.

Oven baked Chicory with Basil
Serves 4

Oven temperature 325 deg. F., Gas No. 3

1 lb. 8 oz. chicory

1 oz. butter

1 teaspoon lemon juice

1 teaspoon caster sugar

$\frac{1}{2}$ teaspoon salt

pepper

$\frac{1}{2}$ teaspoon sweet basil

Blanch chicory in pan of boiling salted water for 2 minutes.
Drain and rinse with cold water. Butter a shallow 2 pint
ovenproof dish with half of the butter. Arrange chicory in

dish, add remaining ingredients and dot with remaining butter. Cover with foil and bake at 325 deg. F., Gas No. 3, for about 1 – 1¼ hours until tender. Lift carefully from dish and serve with juices.

Buttered Fennel Peas and Onions
Serves 4

Oven temperatures 325 deg. F., Gas No. 3

1½ oz. butter	1 teaspoon salt
2 heads fennel	⅛ teaspoon pepper
8 oz. frozen peas	¼ teaspoon ground nutmeg
8 oz. onions, each cut in 6 wedges	6 tablespoons water

Grease a shallow 2½ pint ovenproof dish with ½ oz. of the butter. Separate stems of fennel, slice each in four. Put in dish with other vegetables, seasoning and nutmeg. Dot with remaining butter, add water, cover and bake at 325 deg. F., Gas No. 3, for about 1 hour. Remove lid of dish, cook for further 30 minutes, basting occasionally.

Glazed Sprouts and Chestnuts
Serves 6

8 oz. fresh chestnuts, peeled	1 lb. 8 oz. frozen sprouts
1 chicken stock cube, dissolved in 1 pint water	or 2 lb. fresh sprouts
	salt
1½ oz. butter	¼ teaspoon ground nutmeg

Put chestnuts in a pan with stock, cover and simmer 30 minutes or until tender. Drain. Melt butter in a pan, add chestnuts and brown slowly over medium heat. Cook sprouts in boiling salted water in usual way. Drain and add to chestnuts with nutmeg. Toss together before serving.

Courgettes and Minted Peas
Serves 4

8 oz. courgettes, topped
and tailed

salt

12 oz. packet frozen peas,
thawed

1 teaspoon mint

1 oz. butter

Cut unpeeled courgettes in $\frac{1}{4}$ inch slices or in cubes if large. Put
in a pan of boiling salted water. Add peas and mint. Cover and
simmer about 5 minutes or until just tender. Drain thoroughly.
Return to pan and toss in butter over a low heat.

Vegetable Casserole
Serves 4

Oven temperature 325 deg. F., Gas No. 3

1 large onion

3 courgettes

2 thick slices of marrow,
peeled and cored

8 oz. tomatoes, skinned and
seeds removed

2 green peppers, halved
and seeds removed

3 tablespoons cooking oil

salt

pepper

$\frac{1}{4}$ teaspoon garlic powder

$\frac{1}{2}$ teaspoon whole oregano

$\frac{1}{2}$ teaspoon sweet basil

Slice all the vegetables. Heat oil in large saucepan and fry
onion gently for 2 minutes. Add courgettes and marrow and
cook for 2 − 3 minutes, turning occasionally. Add tomatoes
and peppers and season with salt, pepper, garlic powder,
oregano and sweet basil. Cover pan and cook gently for 1 hour.

Alternatively cook vegetables in a covered casserole in oven
at 325 deg. F., Gas No. 3, for $1\frac{1}{2}$ hours.

Note: If courgettes are unavailable use double quantity of
marrow.

Snacks & Savouries

Spanish Omelette with Oregano

Serves 1

2 medium potatoes, cooked	$\frac{1}{2}$ teaspoon whole oregano
2 medium tomatoes	2 eggs
1 oz. butter	salt
	pepper

Cut potatoes into $\frac{1}{2}$ inch pieces. Skin tomatoes and cut into $\frac{1}{2}$ inch pieces. Melt $\frac{1}{2}$ oz. of the butter in a pan, add potatoes, tomatoes and oregano and cook for 5 minutes. Keep warm.

Beat together eggs and seasoning with a fork until just blended. Heat remaining $\frac{1}{2}$ oz. of butter in a 6 – 7 inch omelette or frying pan over a high heat until sizzling, taking care not to let it burn. Pour egg mixture into pan. Using a fork quickly draw mixture into centre from sides to allow runny egg to cook. Cook until underside is just turning golden brown but centre is still moist, about 1 minute. Slide omelette onto serving plate. Place filling down centre, fold sides of omelette over.
Serve immediately, with green salad.

Haddock and Egg Soufflé

Serves 4

Oven temperature 350 deg. F., Gas No. 4

12 oz. smoked haddock fillet	2 oz. flour
$\frac{1}{2}$ pint plus 5 tablespoons milk	3 eggs, separated
1 whole bay leaf	2 hard-boiled eggs, roughly chopped
$\frac{1}{2}$ teaspoon parsley	1 teaspoon anchovy essence
$\frac{1}{4}$ teaspoon fennel seed	1 teaspoon salt
4 peppercorns	$\frac{1}{8}$ teaspoon pepper
2 oz. butter	

Butter a $1\frac{3}{4}$ pint soufflé dish. Put fish in a pan with milk, herbs and spices, cover and simmer until cooked, about 10 minutes. Remove fish from pan, discard skin and bones. Flake flesh and reserve cooking liquor. Melt butter in a clean pan, blend in flour and cook 1 minute. Gradually add strained cooking liquor and bring to boiling point, stirring. Simmer 2 – 3 minutes then remove from heat. Add blended egg yolks and remaining ingredients, except egg whites. Stir in fish. Whisk egg whites until just stiff and fold into mixture. Turn into prepared dish and bake at 350 deg. F., Gas No. 4, for 45 minutes until well risen and golden brown. Serve immediately.

Ham Omelette with Fine Herbs
Serves 1

2 eggs
$\frac{1}{2}$ teaspoon mixed fine herbs
salt
pepper

$\frac{1}{2}$ oz. butter
2 oz. cooked ham,
cut into $\frac{1}{4}$ inch pieces

Beat eggs, fine herbs, salt and pepper with a fork until just blended. Heat butter in 6 – 7 inch omelette or frying pan over a high heat until sizzling, taking care not to burn it. Pour in egg mixture. Using a fork quickly draw mixture into centre from sides continuously until underside is just turning golden brown, but centre is still moist, about 1 minute.

Place ham across centre of omelette. Fold over one-third away from handle of pan. Remove from heat, shake omelette to edge of pan and turn onto serving plate by turning pan completely over, so making another fold.
Serve immediately.

Soufflé Omelette with Watercress and Chives
Serves 2

4 eggs, separated
2 tablespoons water
$\frac{1}{2}$ teaspoon salt
$\frac{1}{8}$ teaspoon pepper

$\frac{1}{2}$ bunch watercress,
coarsely chopped
2 teaspoons chives
$\frac{1}{2}$ oz. butter

Blend together egg yolks, water and seasoning. Whisk egg whites until they form soft peaks, fold into egg yolks then add watercress and chives. Heat a 9 inch frying pan until piping hot, add butter and, when melted, pour in omelette mixture. Cook gently until underside is golden. Put pan under a medium grill, and cook about 1 minute until top of omelette is set. Fold omelette in half, away from handle. Turn onto serving dish. Serve immediately.

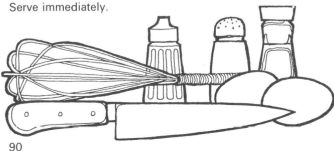

Piquant Cheese Crumb Soufflé

Serves 4

Oven temperature 375 deg. F., Gas No. 5

2 eggs	salt
4 oz. cheese, grated	½ teaspoon cayenne
4 oz. white breadcrumbs	½ pint milk
½ teaspoon mustard powder	

Separate eggs and place yolks in a large bowl. Add cheese, breadcrumbs, mustard, salt and cayenne. Add a little of the milk and beat until well mixed. Stir in remainder of the milk. Whisk egg whites until just stiff and fold carefully into egg yolk mixture. Pour into a buttered 1½ pint soufflé dish and bake at 375 deg. F., Gas No. 5, for 30 – 35 minutes. Serve immediately.

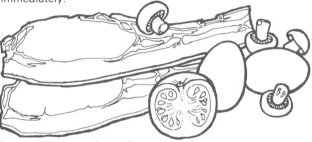

Sunday Supper Oven Fry

Serves 6

Oven temperature 400 deg. F., Gas No. 6

1 teaspoon instant minced onion	6 tomatoes, halved
3 teaspoons water	6 oz. button mushrooms
6 large rashers bacon, de-rinded	1 oz. butter
	6 eggs
Soak onion in water for 10 minutes	

Divide bacon between buttered individual ovenproof entrée dishes. Add two halves of tomatoes, cut side up, in each dish. Remove ends of stalks from mushrooms. Add mushrooms to dishes, stalks upwards, and sprinkle with minced onion. Dot with butter and bake at 400 deg. F., Gas No. 6, about 10 minutes until bacon is beginning to brown lightly at edges. Add an egg to each dish and cook until white is firm, about 5 – 7 minutes. Serve with toast.

Creamy Curried Eggs
Serves 4

1 oz. butter	salt
1 tablespoon curry powder	pepper
1 oz. flour	4 eggs, hard-boiled
$\frac{1}{2}$ pint milk	4 slices buttered toast
3 tablespoons double cream	sprigs of watercress
1 oz. sultanas	

Melt butter in a saucepan. Add curry powder and fry gently for 3 – 4 minutes, stirring continuously. Add flour and continue cooking for 2 minutes. Remove from heat and gradually add milk and cream. Bring to the boil and cook for 2 – 3 minutes, stirring continuously. Add sultanas and check seasoning. Add a little milk if sauce becomes too thick. Cut eggs in half lengthways and place two halves on each piece of buttered toast. Place on oval serving dish and cover eggs with curry sauce. Garnish with sprigs of watercress.

Curry Cream Vol-au-Vent
Serves 6

Oven temperature 425 deg. F., Gas No. 7

2 × 7 oz. packets frozen puff pastry, thawed	pinch cayenne
1 egg, blended with 1 tablespoon water	$\frac{1}{4}$ teaspoon ground ginger
	2 tablespoons mango chutney, finely chopped
Filling	12 oz. cooked turkey or chicken, diced
1$\frac{1}{2}$ oz. butter	
1 large onion, chopped	1 oz. sultanas
1 tablespoon curry powder	5 oz. carton soured cream
1 tablespoon flour	salt
1 chicken stock cube, dissolved in $\frac{1}{2}$ pint water	pepper
	white grapes

Place one rectangle of thawed pastry on top of other. Roll out double their length on a floured board. Fold in three, then roll to an 8 inch square. Cut an 8 inch circle, using a plate as a guide. Place on a baking tray, make a cut $\frac{1}{2}$ inch from edge all way round circle and almost to base of pastry. Chill for 10 minutes in refrigerator then brush top with egg glaze. Bake at 425 deg. F.,

Gas No. 7, about 25 minutes until well risen and golden brown. Carefully remove centre circle for lid. Scrape out uncooked pastry and leave case to cool on a wire tray.

Melt butter for filling in a pan. Add onion, cook until soft but not coloured. Stir in curry powder and flour and cook 1 minute. Blend in stock, cayenne, ginger and mango chutney. Bring to boil, stirring, then simmer 5 minutes. Add turkey or chicken and sultanas. Simmer, uncovered, 5 minutes then blend in soured cream and plenty of seasoning. Reheat pastry case for 5 minutes at 425 deg. F., Gas No. 7, pour in hot turkey mixture and top with lid. Garnish with white grapes.

Kidney Mushroom and Bacon Kebabs
Makes 30

5 lamb's kidneys
10 rashers streaky
bacon, de-rinded
4 oz. button mushrooms

$\frac{1}{4}$ teaspoon ground nutmeg
30 wooden cocktail sticks
cooking oil

Remove fat and membrane from kidneys. Cut each kidney in half. Remove core with scissors. Cut each half in three pieces. Stretch bacon rashers on a board with back of a knife. Cut each in three pieces. Form each piece into a roll. Wash and dry mushrooms, remove a little of stems. Cut mushrooms in half and sprinkle with ground nutmeg. Assemble kebabs with a piece of kidney, a bacon roll and half a mushroom on each cocktail stick. Place on a baking tray. Brush with oil and grill for 10 minutes, turning once. Arrange on a dish and serve hot.

Creamed Celery and Ham

Serves 6

Oven temperature 425 deg. F., Gas No. 7

15 oz. can celery hearts, drained	1 pint milk
	1 teaspoon made mustard
12 slices cooked ham	3 oz. cheese, grated
2 oz. butter	salt
1 onion, chopped	pepper
2 oz. flour	$\frac{1}{2}$ teaspoon ground sage

Divide celery hearts lengthways into 12 equal pieces. Wrap a slice of ham round each celery heart. Arrange on a shallow ovenproof dish. Melt butter in a pan, add onion and cook slowly until soft, but not coloured. Blend in flour, cook 1 minute. Slowly add milk and simmer 2 – 3 minutes, stirring, until thick. Add mustard, most of the cheese, seasoning and sage. Spoon sauce over ham rolls. Sprinkle with remaining cheese. Bake at 425 deg. F., Gas No. 7, for 25 – 30 minutes until brown.

Serve with a green salad.

Spinach with Ham

Serves 4

Oven temperature 425 deg. F., Gas No. 7

2 × 14 oz. packets frozen chopped spinach	$1\frac{1}{2}$ oz. butter
	$1\frac{1}{2}$ oz. flour
1 oz. butter	$\frac{3}{4}$ pint milk
salt	$\frac{1}{2}$ teaspoon ground nutmeg
pepper	3 oz. cheese, grated
8 slices lean ham	

Cook spinach according to directions on the packet. Add butter and season to taste. Divide the spinach into 8 and spoon into the centre of each slice of ham. Roll up and place in a buttered shallow ovenproof dish.

Melt butter in saucepan, add flour and cook gently for 2 – 3 minutes. Remove from heat and gradually add milk. Bring to the boil for 2 – 3 minutes, stirring. Add nutmeg and 2 oz. of grated cheese. Season to taste. Pour over rolls of ham and sprinkle with remaining cheese. Bake at 425 deg. F., Gas No. 7, for 30 minutes until golden brown. Serve immediately.

Creamy Egg and Tomato Flan

Serves 4

Oven temperature 425 deg. F., Gas No. 7

Pastry

6 oz. flour	2 hard-boiled eggs
$\frac{1}{2}$ teaspoon salt	salt
4 oz. butter	pepper
3 tablespoons water	$\frac{1}{4}$ pint double cream
Filling	$\frac{1}{2}$ teaspoon sweet basil
1 onion, chopped	2 oz. cheese, grated
2 tomatoes	sprigs of watercress

Sift flour and salt, rub in 3 oz. of the butter until mixture resembles fine breadcrumbs. Add water and bind to form a stiff dough. Knead lightly and leave to rest in a cool place for 30 minutes. Roll out and use to line an 8 inch plain flan ring. Line with foil and fill with baking beans. Bake 'blind' at 425 deg. F., Gas No. 7, for 15 minutes. Remove foil and beans and continue baking for 7–10 minutes until completely cooked. Cook onion gently in remaining butter for 3–4 minutes. Skin tomatoes and slice. Slice hard-boiled eggs. Arrange onion in base of flan case, top with overlapping hard-boiled egg and slices of tomatoes. Season. Lightly beat cream with basil and pour into flan. Sprinkle with grated cheese. Bake at 425 deg. F., Gas No. 7, for 25–30 minutes.

Garnish with watercress.

Poppy Seed Twists

Makes about 36

Oven temperature 425 deg. F., Gas No. 7

4 oz. plain flour	4 teaspoons water
pinch cayenne	1 teaspoon French mustard
pinch salt	1 teaspoon poppy seed
1 teaspoon paprika	1 tablespoon Parmesan
2 oz. butter	

Sift flour, cayenne, salt and paprika into a bowl. Rub in butter, mix to a dough with water. Roll out thinly on a lightly floured board to a 7" × 9" rectangle. Spread half of surface with mustard then sprinkle with poppy seeds. Fold uncoated half over, press edges to seal. Roll out again to a 7" × 9" rectangle. Cut in half lengthways. Cut into ½ inch wide strips, 3½ inches long. Twist each one and place on a greased baking tray. Bake at 425 deg. F., Gas No. 7, about 10 minutes until crisp and pale golden. Sprinkle with Parmesan cheese. Bake for a further 2 – 3 minutes. Cool on a wire tray then store in an airtight tin.

Dutch Meat Balls
Makes about 36

¼ oz. or 2 teaspoons powdered gelatine

1 beef stock cube, dissolved in ½ pint water

1¼ oz. butter

1¼ oz. flour

6 oz. cooked ham and veal, finely chopped

1 teaspoon parsley

¼ teaspoon ground nutmeg

¼ teaspoon onion powder

salt

pepper

1 egg, beaten

3 oz. browned breadcrumbs

oil or fat for deep frying

Dissolve gelatine with stock in a bowl over a pan of simmering water. Remove from heat. Melt butter in a pan, blend in flour and cook 1 minute then stir in stock. Bring to boiling point, stirring, and simmer 2 minutes. Add meat, parsley, nutmeg, onion powder and plenty of seasoning. Turn onto a plate, cover and leave in a cold place for several hours or overnight until set. Roll into small balls. Brush with egg and coat with bread-crumbs. Fry in hot oil or fat until golden brown. Serve hot with mild mustard.

This is a Dutch speciality, often served with drinks. The outsides are crisp, while the insides remain soft.

Devils on Horseback
Makes 14

7½ oz. can prunes, drained

4 oz. liver sausage

½ teaspoon mixed fine herbs

7 rashers streaky bacon, de-rinded

cocktail sticks

Remove stones from prunes. Blend together liver sausage and fine herbs. Form into small sausages, use to fill prunes. Stretch bacon rashers on a board with back of a knife. Cut each in half. Wrap each prune in a rasher of bacon. Secure with a wooden cocktail stick. Grill about 6 minutes until bacon is crisp, turning once. Serve hot.

Ham and Cheese Pizza

Serves 6

Oven temperature 400 deg. F., Gas No. 6

8 oz. self-raising flour

1 teaspoon baking powder

$\frac{1}{2}$ teaspoon salt

2 oz. margarine

1 egg, beaten

5 tablespoons milk

12 oz. tomatoes, skinned and thinly sliced

salt

pepper

1 teaspoon mixed fine herbs

6 oz. cooked ham cut as 1 thick slice

3 oz. Gruyère or Emmenthal cheese

$\frac{1}{2}$ oz. butter, melted

8 black olives

Sift flour, baking powder and salt into a bowl, and rub in margarine, add beaten egg and milk and mix to form a soft dough. Roll out to a round, 10 inches in diameter. Place on a greased baking tray and tuck under a $\frac{3}{4}$ inch border. Arrange slices of tomato over top of the pizza. Season with salt and pepper, and sprinkle over fine herbs. Cut ham slice into $\frac{1}{2}$ inch wide strips and arrange on tomato. Slice cheese very thinly and arrange between ham. Brush well with melted butter and bake at 400 deg. F., Gas No. 6, for about 30 minutes. Garnish with black olives and serve hot, cut into wedges.

Celery Cheese Puffs

Makes 24

Oven temperature 425 deg. F., Gas No. 7

$13\frac{1}{2}$ oz. packet frozen puff pastry, thawed

6 oz. Cheddar cheese, finely grated

$\frac{1}{4}$ teaspoon celery salt

1 egg, beaten

Divide pastry into 2. Roll out each piece to about a 12" × 15" oblong and cut out 12 rounds from each with a plain $3\frac{1}{2}$ inch cutter.

Mix together grated cheese and celery salt. Divide equally between pastry rounds. Brush edges with beaten egg, gather up edges and seal firmly in the centre. Turn over and roll to flatten. Place on a baking tray and make 3 cuts on the top of each. Glaze with beaten egg and bake at 425 deg. F., Gas No. 7, for 15 – 20 minutes until golden brown. Serve hot.

Cheese and Bacon Cayenne Tartlets

Serves 4

Oven temperature 400 deg. F., Gas No. 6

6 oz. plain flour
½ teaspoon salt
4 oz. butter
3 tablespoons water
4 oz. streaky bacon, de-rinded

1 oz. flour
½ pint milk
2 oz. cheese, grated
¼ teaspoon cayenne (less for a milder taste)
stuffed olives

Sift flour and salt together. Rub in 3 oz. of the butter until mixture resembles fine breadcrumbs. Add water and bind together to form a stiff dough. Knead lightly and leave to rest for 10 minutes. Roll out to ¼ inch thickness and cut out 12 rounds with 3½ inch plain cutter. Place in deep 2½ inch patty tins. Bake at 400 deg. F., Gas No. 6, for 10 – 15 minutes until golden brown.

Cut bacon into ½ inch pieces. Fry gently in frying pan until crisp. Remove and drain on kitchen paper. Melt remaining butter in a saucepan, stir in flour and cook 2 – 3 minutes. Remove from heat and gradually stir in milk. Bring to boil and cook for 2 – 3 minutes, stirring continuously. Add bacon, cheese and cayenne. Fill tartlet cases with sauce and garnish with slices of stuffed olives. Serve hot or cold.

Swiss Cheese Fondue
Serves 6

4 glasses dry white wine

$\frac{1}{4}$ teaspoon instant minced garlic

1 lb. Emmenthal or Gruyère cheese, grated

1 oz. cornflour

salt

pepper

1 tablespoon kirsch

Pour all but 3 tablespoons of wine into a thick pan. Add garlic and cheese. Heat very slowly until cheese has melted. Do not allow the mixture to boil. Blend cornflour with remaining wine in a small bowl until smooth. Add a little of the hot cheese mixture to cornflour. Return to rest of cheese in pan. Bring to boiling point, stirring constantly, until thick. Add salt, pepper and kirsch. Serve with 1 inch French bread cubes to dip in hot fondue. Use forks to spear the bread.

Note This Swiss dish is very filling so you will only need one other savoury — not cheese — to accompany it if you are serving it with drinks. Let your guests serve themselves but provide plenty of paper napkins for mopping up.

Sausage Rolls with Herbs
Makes 18

Oven temperature 450 deg. F., Gas No. 8

7 oz. packet frozen puff pastry, thawed

Filling

8 oz. pork sausage meat

$\frac{1}{4}$ teaspoon marjoram

$\frac{1}{4}$ teaspoon thyme

$\frac{1}{4}$ teaspoon onion salt

ground black pepper

Glaze

1 egg, blended with 1 tablespoon water

Mix together sausage meat, herbs and seasonings for filling. Roll out pastry to a 12" × 9" rectangle then cut into three strips, each 12" × 3". Divide sausage meat in 3 equal portions and roll out to form 3 rolls, each 12 inches long. Place one on top of one strip of pastry, damp down one long edge of pastry with water. Fold pastry over filling and seal underneath. Repeat with other two lengths of pastry and sausage. Cut long rolls in 2 inch lengths with a sharp knife. Make 2 or 3 cuts with a knife on top of each roll. Place rolls on a damp baking tray. Brush with egg glaze then bake at 450 deg. F., Gas No. 8, for 10 minutes. Reduce heat to 400 deg. F., Gas No. 6, and bake for a further 10 minutes.

Prawn Quiches

Serves 4

Oven temperature 425 deg. F., Gas No. 7

Pastry

4 oz. plain flour

$\frac{1}{4}$ teaspoon salt

2 oz. butter

1 – 2 tablespoons water

Filling

1 small onion,
finely chopped

$\frac{1}{2}$ oz. butter

2 oz. fresh or frozen
peeled prawns

1 teaspoon barbecue
seasoning

2 eggs

$\frac{1}{4}$ pint single cream

salt

pepper

4 teaspoons Parmesan

sprigs of parsley

Sift together flour and salt. Rub in butter until mixture resembles fine breadcrumbs. Add water to bind to a stiff dough, knead lightly and leave to rest for 30 minutes. Roll out thinly and line 4 individual fluted tartlet tins, $4\frac{1}{2}$ inches in diameter and 1 inch deep. Line with foil and fill with beans. Bake at 425 deg. F., Gas No. 7, for 10 minutes. Remove foil and beans and continue baking for 5 minutes. Reduce oven temperature to 325 deg. F., Gas No. 3. Cook onion gently in butter for 3 – 4 minutes until soft but not coloured. Remove from heat, add prawns and barbecue seasoning. Divide between tartlet cases. Beat eggs with cream, season, and strain. Pour equal amounts into tartlet cases. Sprinkle top of each with a teaspoon of Parmesan cheese. Bake at 325 deg. F., Gas No. 3, for 30 – 35 minutes until set. Serve hot or cold garnished with sprigs of parsley.

Hot Kipper Toasts

Serves 4

4 large slices white bread

6 oz. packet frozen
kipper fillets, thawed

2 oz. butter

$\frac{1}{4}$ teaspoon garlic pepper

1 teaspoon lemon juice

4 lemon wedges

Toast bread on one side only. Place kipper fillets on untoasted side of bread, trimming so that bread is completely covered. Blend together butter, garlic pepper and lemon juice. Spread on kipper fillets and grill for 3 – 4 minutes. Cut each slice into 3 fingers and serve with lemon wedges.

Welsh Rarebit

Serves 4

½ oz. butter
½ oz. flour
6 tablespoons milk
4 oz. cheese, grated
salt
pepper

pinch cayenne
¼ teaspoon ground nutmeg
½ teaspoon made mustard
4 large slices toast,
buttered

Melt butter in a pan, blend in flour and cook 1 minute. Blend in milk, bring to boiling point and cook for 2 minutes, stirring. Add most of cheese, seasoning, cayenne, nutmeg and mustard. Heat gently until cheese has melted. Divide mixture between slices of toast. Sprinkle remaining cheese on top then cook under grill for a few minutes until golden brown. Cut each slice in quarters and serve at once.

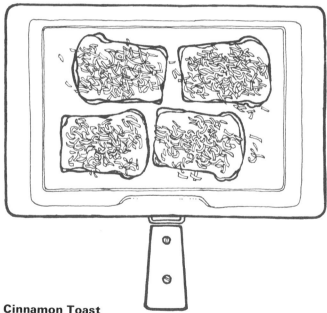

Cinnamon Toast

Toast bread in the usual way, spread generously with butter. Sprinkle lightly with cinnamon and then with caster or demerara sugar. Serve immediately while hot.

Puddings hot & cold

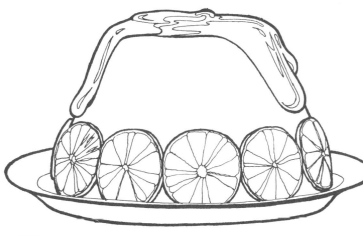

Bread and Butter Pudding with Dates

Serves 4

Oven temperature 350 deg. F., Gas No. 4

2 eggs

1 oz. sugar

1 pint milk

½ teaspoon
ground nutmeg

8 thin slices white bread

2 oz. butter

3 oz. stoned dates,
roughly chopped

demerara sugar

Beat eggs and sugar until frothy. Gradually add hot but not boiling milk. Add nutmeg. Remove crusts from bread. Butter bread and cut each slice into 4. Arrange squares of bread evenly in layers in a 2 pint pie dish adding a few chopped dates to each layer. Strain over egg custard and leave for 15 minutes. Sprinkle with demerara sugar, stand dish in a roasting pan of water, and bake at 350 deg. F., Gas No. 4, for 30 minutes until custard is just set.

Cinnamon Apricot Charlotte

Serves 4 – 6

Oven temperature 400 deg. F., Gas No. 6

1 lb. 3 oz. can apricots

3 oz. demerara sugar

grated rind and juice of
½ lemon

½ teaspoon cinnamon

small sliced brown loaf,
with crusts removed

4 oz. unsalted butter,
melted

Grease a 7 inch sponge sandwich tin. Drain apricots, reserve 2 tablespoons juice. Put apricots in a pan with reserved juice, 2 oz. sugar, lemon rind and juice and cinnamon. Cook over low heat until soft, mashing the mixture with a wooden spoon. Leave to cool. Cut bread in long strips. Cover base and sides of tin with some of the bread. Sprinkle with half of the remaining sugar and pour over half of the melted butter. Add apricot pulp. Cover apricot with single layer of bread. Pour over rest of butter and sprinkle with remaining sugar. Place on a baking tray and bake at 400 deg. F., Gas No. 6, for about 45 minutes. Cool slightly then turn out onto a serving dish.

Old Fashioned Christmas Pudding

Fills two 1½ pint basins

4 oz. self-raising flour

½ teaspoon mixed spice

¼ teaspoon ground nutmeg

½ teaspoon salt

8 oz. currants

8 oz. sultanas

8 oz. stoned raisins

6 oz. fresh white breadcrumbs

6 oz. suet, finely chopped

2 oz. candied peel, finely chopped

1 oz. almonds, blanched and chopped

1 small cooking apple, peeled, cored and grated

grated rind and juice of 1 orange

8 oz. soft brown sugar

3 eggs, beaten

5 tablespoons port

Put all ingredients except eggs and port into a large bowl and toss until well mixed. Add eggs and port and stir until all ingredients are thoroughly blended. Turn into two 1½ pint greased pudding basins. Cover tops with greaseproof paper and foil. Simmer or steam puddings 6 – 8 hours. Lift puddings out of pans and leave covered to cool. Store in a cool place until needed. Simmer 3 hours before serving.

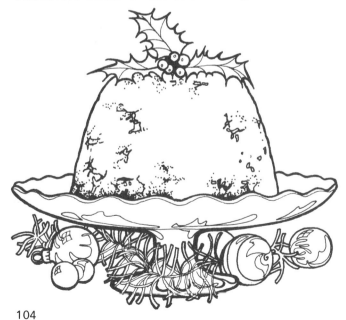

Danish Apple Layer
Serves 6

2 lb. 8 oz. cooking apples, peeled, cored and sliced
thinly peeled rind and juice of 1 large lemon
3 whole cloves
¼ teaspoon cinnamon
3 oz. sultanas
6 oz. granulated sugar

3 oz. butter, melted
6 oz. digestive biscuits, crushed
2 oz. demerara sugar
1 oz. ratafias
¼ pint double cream, whipped

Simmer apple with flavourings, sultanas and granulated sugar in covered pan, until tender. Remove lid and simmer until thick but not puréed. Remove lemon rind and cloves, leave until cold. Mix melted butter with biscuits and demerara sugar. An hour or so before serving spread half of apple mixture in base of a 7 inch diameter glass dish. Cover with half of crushed biscuit mixture. Repeat with remaining apple and biscuits. Decorate with whipped cream and ratafias. Serve chilled, with pouring cream.

Plum Crumble
Serves 4
Oven temperature 400 deg. F., Gas No. 6

1 lb. 8 oz. plums, stoned
4 oz. caster sugar
4 tablespoons water

Crumble
4 oz. plain flour
¼ teaspoon ground ginger
2 oz. butter
2 oz. caster sugar
2 oz. ginger biscuits, crushed

Put plums in a 2½ pint ovenproof dish. Add sugar and water. Bake at 400 deg. F., Gas No. 6, for 10 minutes. Sift flour and ginger into a bowl. Rub in butter until mixture resembles breadcrumbs. Stir in sugar and ginger biscuit crumbs. Remove dish from oven. Sprinkle crumble mix over top. Return to oven and bake for a further 30 minutes or until golden brown.

Cinnamon and Walnut Cherry Tart

Serves 4 – 6

Oven temperature 375 deg. F., Gas No. 5

Pastry

3 oz. plain flour

1 teaspoon cinnamon

$1\frac{1}{2}$ oz. sugar

$\frac{1}{2}$ teaspoon salt

2 oz. butter

2 oz. walnuts

1 egg yolk, beaten with
2 teaspoons water

Filling

1 lb. can black cherries,
pitted

$\frac{1}{2}$ oz. cornflour, blended
with 1 tablespoon water

Sift flour, cinnamon, sugar and salt into a bowl. Rub in butter until mixture resembles fine breadcrumbs. Add grated, or very finely chopped walnuts. Gradually add egg yolk and water and bind together to a soft dough. Knead very lightly. Leave to rest in a cool place for 10 minutes. Roll out pastry to a round, large enough to line a 7 inch fluted flan ring. Place ring on a baking tray and line with pastry. Line with foil and fill with baking beans and bake at 375 deg. F., Gas No. 5, for 15 minutes. Remove foil with beans and flan ring and continue baking for 5 – 7 minutes until golden brown and crisp. Cool.

Drain juice from cherries into a saucepan, add blended cornflour and bring to the boil for 2 – 3 minutes, stirring continuously. Add cherries and leave to cool. Place flan case on serving plate and fill with cherry mixture. Serve with whipped cream.

Spiced Banana Turnovers

Serves 6

Oven temperature 425 deg. F., Gas No. 7

$7\frac{1}{2}$ oz. packet frozen puff
pastry, thawed

3 bananas

2 oz. raisins

1 teaspoon ground nutmeg

1 teaspoon ground ginger

2 tablespoons lemon juice

2 tablespoons apricot jam

1 egg, beaten with
1 tablespoon water

Roll out pastry to an oblong 12″ × 8″ and cut 6 squares of 4 inches. Dice bananas and add raisins, mix with nutmeg, ginger, lemon juice and apricot jam. Divide between pastry squares. Brush edges well with egg and water and seal by bringing each edge up to a central point. Flute the sealed edges. Brush well with beaten egg and bake at 425 deg. F., Gas No. 7, for 20 – 25 minutes until golden brown.

Serve hot or cold with cream.

Blackcurrant Plate Pie

Serves 6

Oven temperature 400 deg. F., Gas No. 6

Shortcrust pastry
10 oz. plain flour
$\frac{1}{4}$ teaspoon salt
3 oz. butter
2 oz. lard
about 3 – 4 tablespoons
cold water

Filling
4 oz. caster sugar
1 oz. cornflour
$\frac{1}{4}$ pint water
1 lb. fresh or frozen
blackcurrants
$\frac{1}{2}$ teaspoon mixed spice

Glaze
little milk
caster sugar

Grease an 8 inch enamel pie plate. Sift flour and salt and rub in fats until mixture resembles fine breadcrumbs. Add water and bind to a stiff dough. Knead lightly and leave in a cool place while preparing filling.

Put sugar and cornflour for filling in a pan, blend in water and bring to boiling point. Simmer 2 minutes, stirring. Add blackcurrants and spice, leave until cold. Line pie plate with half of pastry. Spoon in filling. Cover with remaining pastry, seal and make a pattern round edge with a fork. Brush top of pie with milk, sprinkle with caster sugar and bake at 400 deg. F., Gas No. 6, for about 40 minutes or until pale golden brown.

Apple and Lemon Flan

Serves 6

Oven temperature 275 deg. F., Gas No. 1

Flan Case
6 oz. digestive biscuits, crushed
3 oz. butter, melted
1 oz. caster sugar

Filling
$\frac{1}{4}$ pint double cream
6 oz. can condensed milk
finely grated rind and juice of 2 large lemons
5 oz. can apple sauce
$\frac{1}{2}$ teaspoon apple pie spice

Blend together flan case ingredients. Turn into a 9 inch oven-proof glass flan dish. Press biscuit mixture round base and sides of dish with back of a spoon. Bake at 275 deg. F., Gas No. 1, for 8 minutes. Remove from oven and leave to cool. Mix together cream, condensed milk and lemon rind for filling. Beat in lemon juice, apple sauce, and spice. Pour into flan case and leave in refrigerator to set. Serve with lightly whipped cream.

Ginger and Mandarin Flan

Serves 4 – 6

1 oz. custard powder
$\frac{3}{4}$ teaspoon ground ginger
2 oz. sugar
$\frac{1}{4}$ pint milk
$\frac{1}{4}$ pint double cream

11 oz. can mandarin oranges
7 inch baked pastry flan case
1 piece stem ginger

Mix custard powder, $\frac{1}{4}$ teaspoon ground ginger, 1 tablespoon sugar and a little of the milk together in a bowl. Bring remaining milk to the boil then gradually stir into custard mixture. Return to pan and cook, stirring, until thick. Cover and leave to cool, whisking occasionally. Whip cream until just stiff and fold half of it into the custard. Drain mandarin juice into a saucepan with the remaining ground ginger and sugar. Boil rapidly until syrupy and reduced by half. Spread custard into flan case, arrange mandarin slices on top and glaze with the juice. Pipe or spoon remaining cream round the edge and decorate with thin slices of stem ginger.

Flamed Mandarin Pancakes
Serves 6

Oven temperature 375 deg. F., Gas No. 5

Pancake Batter	*Filling*
4 oz. plain flour	2 × 11 oz. cans mandarin oranges
pinch of salt	
2 teaspoons cinnamon	$\frac{1}{2}$ oz. cornflour
1 egg, beaten	*Meringue*
$\frac{1}{2}$ pint milk	2 egg whites
oil or lard for frying	4 oz. caster sugar
	1 − 2 tablespoons Grand Marnier

Sift flour, salt and cinnamon into a bowl. Make a well in the centre and drop in beaten egg. Using a whisk or wooden spoon gradually work flour into the egg with half the milk. Beat well until smooth then beat in remaining milk. Pour into a jug. Heat a little oil in a 7 inch frying pan. Pour in enough batter to thinly coat base of the pan, cook until underside is golden brown. Turn and cook on other side. Place on a plate and keep warm. Make 8 pancakes with the batter.

Drain mandarins, reserving $\frac{1}{2}$ pint of the juice. Blend a little juice with cornflour then blend in remaining juice. Bring to the boil and cook, stirring, until thickened. Cool slightly and stir in fruit. Use to sandwich the 8 pancakes, piling them up to make a 'cake', on an ovenproof serving plate.

Whisk egg whites until very stiff and dry. Whisk in sugar and continue beating until stiff. Warm Grand Marnier gently in a pan. Pour over pancakes and 'flame' them. Cover pancakes completely with meringue. Swirl up with a knife and bake at 375 deg. F., Gas No. 5, for about 20 minutes until golden brown. Serve immediately.

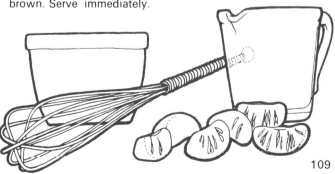

Chilled Fruit Caramel

Serves 4

Oven temperature 300 deg. F., Gas No. 2

1 lb. prepared fruit, e.g. pears, bananas, peaches, all peeled and sliced

thinly peeled rind and juice of 1 orange

2 – 3 oz. granulated sugar

½ teaspoon cinnamon

3 eggs, beaten

Caramel

2 tablespoons water

2 oz. granulated sugar

Decoration

¼ pint double cream, lightly whipped

½ oz. blanched, shredded almonds, lightly toasted

Put prepared fruit, orange rind, juice, sugar and cinnamon in a pan. Simmer gently 5 – 10 minutes, until fruit is tender, then remove from heat. Put water and sugar for caramel in a heavy pan, dissolve slowly then bring to boiling point and boil until deep golden brown. Pour caramel into a 1½ pint pudding basin and use to coat base and sides. Strain eggs onto fruit mixture and mix well. Pour into prepared basin. Place in a meat pan half-filled with hot water. Bake at 300 deg. F., Gas No. 2, for about 1 hour or until just set. Leave in refrigerator overnight, turn out onto a serving plate. Cover with cream and spike with almonds.

Spiced Gooseberry Cream
Serves 6

1 lb. 8 oz. gooseberries,
topped and tailed
5 oz. caster sugar
½ teaspoon mixed spice
4 tablespoons water

thinly peeled rind of 1 lemon
½ pint double cream,
lightly whipped
¼ pint thick custard
few drops green colouring

Put gooseberries in a pan with sugar, spice, water and lemon rind. Cover and simmer until fruit is soft. Discard lemon rind, sieve fruit or purée in a blender. Put purée on one side to cool. Mix together cream and custard, fold into cold purée. Add colouring, if necessary. Spoon into individual dishes and chill before serving.

Summer Red Pudding
Serves 6

1 lb. 8 oz. mixed soft fruit, e.g.
raspberries
whitecurrants
redcurrants
8 oz. cooking apple, peeled
cored and diced
6 oz. caster sugar

Topping
1½ oz. butter, melted
3 oz. digestive biscuits,
crushed
1 oz. ground almonds
1½ oz. demerara sugar
½ teaspoon ground allspice
1 packet sponge fingers
icing sugar

Butter a 7 inch soufflé dish. Put fruit in pan with sugar, cover and simmer gently until fruit is very soft. Sieve, or purée in a blender, then leave to cool. Mix together ingredients for topping except sponge fingers, put half in dish and press down with back of a spoon. Cut each sponge finger in half, arrange close together round edge of dish with rounded sides outwards and rounded edge of each finger at top. Pour in fruit mixture, sprinkle with remaining topping. Leave in refrigerator overnight. Dust top with little icing sugar, serve with whipped cream.

Ginger Choc Parfait
Serves 6 – 8

1 pint packet instant
vanilla pudding
1 pint packet instant
chocolate pudding

2 pints milk
1 teaspoon ground ginger
2 pieces crystallised
ginger

Make up puddings as directed on the packets. Stir ground ginger into the vanilla pudding. In tall glasses make alternate layers of vanilla and chocolate allowing each layer a minute or two to set. Chill. Decorate with slivers of crystallised ginger.

Cinnamon Pears in Wine
Serves 6

$\frac{1}{2}$ pint red wine
$\frac{1}{2}$ pint water
4 oz. granulated sugar

$\frac{1}{2}$ teaspoon cinnamon
1 strip lemon peel
12 pears

Put all ingredients except pears in a large pan, heat without boiling until sugar has dissolved. Peel pears, leaving stalks on. Remove eye from base of each pear. Add pears to pan. Cover and simmer very slowly, basting frequently, for 30 minutes or until pears are tender. Remove pears from pan and put in a serving dish. Boil wine mixture for a few minutes until it is slightly syrupy. Strain over pears. Leave in a cold place until just before serving. Serve with chilled single cream.

Spiced Summer Pudding
Serves 6

2 lb. soft fruit to include any of these:
strawberries
raspberries
blackcurrants
redcurrants
stoned cherries
blackberries
4 tablespoons water
8 – 10 oz. caster sugar
$\frac{1}{4}$ teaspoon mixed spice
7 – 8 thin slices of bread, with crusts removed

Put fruit in a pan with water, sugar and spice. Cover and simmer gently until fruit begins to soften. Line a 1½ pint pudding basin with bread. Make sure the base and sides of basin are completely covered with bread. Half fill dish with fruit. Cover with a single layer of bread. Add rest of fruit and some juice. Cover with a lid of bread. Place a plate, which just fits inside top of basin, over bread and put weights on top of plate. Leave in a cold place overnight and until needed. Just before serving, loosen round edge with a knife. Turn out onto a flat plate. Serve with whipped cream and caster sugar.

Hazelnut Cherry Ice Cream
Serves 6

½ pint double cream
¼ pint single cream
3 oz. icing sugar
½ teaspoon ground allspice
2 eggs, separated

2 oz. hazelnuts, skins
removed, chopped
2 oz. glacé cherries,
chopped

Whip double cream until stiff and gradually whisk in single
cream. Sieve together sugar and ground allspice and stir into
cream with two egg yolks. Whisk whites until just stiff and fold
in. Fold in nuts and cherries and spoon into 2 lb. loaf tin or 2 pint
container. Freeze until hard.

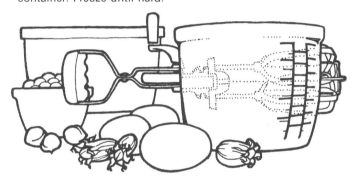

Spiced Orange and Pineapple Glory
Serves 4

3 oranges, peeled and sliced
12 oz. can pineapple chunks
1 teaspoon arrowroot
¼ teaspoon ground allspice

12 baby meringues,
lightly crushed
½ pint double cream,
whipped

Arrange some of the orange slices around the insides of 4 tall
glasses, reserving one slice for decoration. Roughly chop remaining orange. Strain pineapple juice into a saucepan. Blend a
little of the juice with arrowroot and allspice, mix into the pan and
bring to the boil, stirring. Add pineapple chunks and remaining
orange pieces and leave to cool. Divide pineapple mixture
between the glasses and chill. Just before serving fold crushed
meringues into whipped cream and pile on top of fruit. Cut
remaining slice of orange into 4 and place a piece on the top of
each glass.

Black Cherry Pavlovas
Serves 6

Oven temperature 300 deg. F., Gas No. 2

3 egg whites
6 oz. caster sugar
$\frac{1}{4}$ teaspoon vinegar
$\frac{1}{4}$ teaspoon vanilla essence
2 teaspoons cornflour
16 oz. can black cherries, pitted

2 teaspoons arrowroot
$\frac{1}{2}$ teaspoon ground allspice
$\frac{1}{2}$ pint double cream, whipped
$\frac{1}{2}$ oz. flaked almonds, toasted

Cover two baking trays with silicone paper or lightly greased foil and mark on twelve 4 inch circles.

Whisk egg whites till very stiff and dry. Whisk in sugar, half at a time, then add vinegar and vanilla essence and fold in cornflour. Pipe or spread meringue over circles. Bake at 300 deg. F., Gas No. 2, for 1 hour. Turn off oven and leave to cool in oven. Remove carefully from baking trays.

Drain cherries and reserve $\frac{1}{4}$ pint of the juice. Blend arrowroot and allspice with a little of the juice in a small pan then blend in remaining juices. Bring to the boil, stirring, until thickened and clear. Add cherries, reserving 6 for decoration, and leave to cool.

To make up spread 6 of the pavlovas with half of the cream. Spoon cherry mixture on top of cream and cover with second pavlova. Pipe a whirl of cream on top, place a cherry in the centre of each and decorate with flaked almonds.

Pears in Anise Seed Caramel
Serves 4

4 hard eating pears
1 pint water

$\frac{1}{2}$ teaspoon anise seed
4 oz. sugar

Leaving stalks on pears, cut a thin slice from the bottom so that they stand upright. Carefully peel down pears, to remove skin. Place water, anise seed and sugar into a deep saucepan. Cook gently until the sugar has dissolved. Place pears in syrup, cover and poach gently for about 30 minutes, until soft. Remove pears from syrup and place upright in a deep serving dish. Strain syrup and bring to the boil. Continue cooking until syrup caramelises to a golden brown colour at 356 deg. F. Pour immediately over the pears and leave until quite cold before serving. Serve with unwhipped cream.

Breads
Cakes &
Cookies

Soul Scones

Makes 14

Oven temperature 425 deg. F., Gas No. 7

8 oz. plain flour
1 teaspoon ground allspice
2 teaspoons cream of tartar
1 teaspoon bicarbonate
of soda
½ teaspoon salt

1½ oz. butter
¼ teaspoon anise seed
2 oz. caster sugar
4 tablespoons milk
4 tablespoons soda water

Sift together flour, allspice, cream of tartar, bicarbonate of soda and salt. Rub in butter and add anise seed and sugar. Add milk and soda water to bind to a soft dough. Knead lightly and roll out to ½ inch thickness. Cut out scones with a 2 inch plain cutter. Re-roll trimmings and cut out remaining rounds. Place on a greased baking tray and brush tops with extra milk. Bake at 425 deg. F., Gas No. 7, for 10 minutes.

Fine Herb Wholemeal Scones

Makes 16

Oven temperature 425 deg. F., Gas No. 7

¼ pint milk
2 teaspoons mixed fine herbs
4 oz. plain flour
½ teaspoon salt
⅛ teaspoon cayenne
1 teaspoon bicarbonate
of soda

2 teaspoons cream
of tartar
2 oz. wholemeal flour
2 oz. butter
a little extra milk for
glazing
1 oz. cracked wheat

Heat milk and fine herbs until warm, then leave to cool. Sift flour, salt, cayenne, bicarbonate of soda and cream of tartar. Add wholemeal flour and rub in butter until mixture resembles fine breadcrumbs. Add milk and fine herbs and bind to a soft dough. Knead gently and roll out to ½ inch thickness on a lightly floured surface. Cut out scones with a 1½ inch plain cutter. Re-roll trimmings and cut out remaining rounds. Place on a greased baking tray. Brush tops with a little milk and sprinkle with cracked wheat. Bake at 425 deg. F., Gas No. 7, for 10 minutes.

Nutmeg Honey Cakes

Makes 12

Oven temperature 425 deg. F., Gas No. 7

8 oz. plain flour
$\frac{1}{2}$ teaspoon salt
4 teaspoons baking powder
1 teaspoon ground nutmeg

3 oz. butter
4 tablespoons clear honey, warmed
1 – 2 teaspoons milk

Sift together flour, salt, baking powder and nutmeg. Rub in fat until mixture resembles fine breadcrumbs. Gradually add warmed honey, to form a stiff dough. Add extra milk if necessary. Knead lightly. Roll out to $\frac{1}{4}$ inch thickness and cut out rounds with a 2 inch plain cutter. Re-roll trimmings and cut out more rounds. Place on a greased baking tray and bake at 425 deg. F., Gas No. 7, for 15 – 20 minutes.

Serve with butter.

Blackberry Mace Shortcake

Makes 8 slices

Oven temperature 375 deg. F., Gas No. 5

6 oz. self-raising flour
2 oz. cornflour
$\frac{1}{4}$ teaspoon salt
$\frac{1}{2}$ teaspoon ground mace
3 oz. butter
3 oz. sugar

1 egg, beaten
1 – 2 tablespoons milk
$\frac{1}{4}$ pint double cream
12 oz. blackberries, sprinkled with sugar if necessary

Sift flours, salt and mace. Rub in butter until mixture resembles fine breadcrumbs. Add sugar. Add beaten egg, a little at a time, until mixture begins to bind. Add extra milk if necessary to form a fairly stiff dough. Knead lightly and divide the mixture into two.

Press mixture into 2 greased 8 inch sandwich tins, making the tops as smooth as possible. Bake at 375 deg. F., Gas No. 5, for 15 – 20 minutes. Remove and, after 2 minutes, turn out carefully onto a wire tray.

Whisk cream until stiff. Spread two-thirds of it onto one of the shortcakes. Arrange all but 8 of the blackberries on top of the cream and cover with the remaining shortcake. Spoon or pipe remainder of cream onto the top in 8 whirls. Place a blackberry on the centre of each whirl of cream.

Cherry Custard Tarts

Makes 4

Oven temperature 425 deg. F., Gas No. 7

Pastry
4 oz. plain flour
½ teaspoon salt
2 oz. butter
2 tablespoons water

Filling
3 eggs

2 oz. sugar
½ pint milk
1 teaspoon ground nutmeg
¼ pint double cream
16 oz. can black cherries, pitted and drained

Sift together flour and salt. Rub in butter until mixture resembles fine breadcrumbs. Add water and bind together to form a stiff dough. Knead lightly and leave to rest in a cool place for 30 minutes. Roll out and cut 4 rounds with a saucer. Use to line 4 fluted tartlet tins, 4 inches in diameter.

Beat eggs and sugar until well mixed. Pour on hot but not boiling milk. Strain into a jug and stir in nutmeg. Divide equally between each tart. Bake at 425 deg. F., Gas No. 7, for 10 minutes, then reduce temperature of oven to 300 deg. F., Gas No. 2, for 30 minutes until custard sets. Cool. Whisk cream until just stiff. Place in a piping bag, fitted with a small star nozzle, and pipe rosettes of cream round the outside edge of each tart. Pile cherries in centre of tarts.

Pineapple and Cherry Slices

Makes 12 slices

Oven temperature 425 deg. F., Gas No. 7

Pastry

8 oz. plain flour

½ teaspoon salt

4 oz. butter

3 tablespoons water

Sponge

5 oz. self-raising flour

2 teaspoons ground allspice

4 oz. butter

2 oz. soft brown sugar

2 eggs, beaten

2 oz. walnuts, chopped

7 oz. can pineapple, drained and roughly chopped

3 tablespoons pineapple juice

1½ oz. glacé cherries, chopped

2 tablespoons black treacle

Sift together flour and salt. Rub in butter until mixture resembles fine breadcrumbs. Add water to bind to a stiff dough. Knead lightly and leave to rest for 30 minutes. Line a 7" × 11" × 1" tin with a strip of foil for easy removal of pastry after baking. Roll out pastry thinly and line tin. Line pastry with foil and fill with beans. Bake at 425 deg. F., Gas No. 7, for 15 minutes. Remove foil and beans, and continue cooking for 7 minutes until just golden brown. Remove from oven. Reduce temperature to 350 deg. F., Gas No. 4. Sift together flour and allspice. Beat butter and sugar until light and creamy. Gradually add beaten egg, beating well. Add a tablespoon of flour with last addition of egg. Fold in nuts, pineapple pieces, pineapple juice, cherries and treacle. Carefully fold in flour and allspice. Pour into pastry case and bake at 350 deg. F., Gas No. 4, for 1 hour. Remove from tin with foil strip and cool on wire tray.

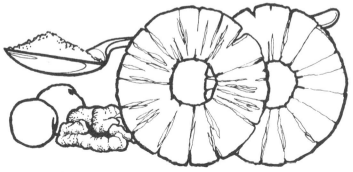

American Apple Strudel

Serves 6

Oven temperature 400 deg. F., Gas No. 6

9 oz. packet frozen puff pastry, thawed

1 lb. 8 oz. cooking apples, peeled, cored and sliced

2 oz. caster sugar

2 oz. sultanas

1 teaspoon apple pie spice

$\frac{1}{2}$ oz. butter

Roll pastry out paper thin on lightly floured board to a 21 inch square. Mix together apples, sugar, sultanas and apple pie spice and spread over two-thirds of pastry. Roll up pastry from end covered with apples. Lift carefully onto an ungreased baking tray, with pastry join underneath. Shape into a horseshoe to fit on baking tray. Melt butter in a pan. Brush top of strudel with butter. Bake at 400 deg. F., Gas No. 6, about 30 minutes until golden brown. Serve hot, in thick slices, sprinkled with caster or icing sugar.

Ginger and Walnut Teabread

Makes about 8 slices

Oven temperature 350 deg. F., Gas No. 4

8 oz. self-raising flour

$\frac{1}{4}$ teaspoon salt

2 teaspoons ground ginger

1 teaspoon baking powder

2 oz. butter

2 oz. sugar

3 oz. walnuts, chopped

1 oz. crystallised ginger, finely chopped

1 egg, beaten

$\frac{1}{4}$ pint milk

1 teaspoon demerara sugar

Sift together flour, salt, ginger and baking powder. Rub in butter until mixture resembles fine breadcrumbs. Mix in sugar, walnuts and crystallised ginger. Mix most of the beaten egg with the milk and add to flour and butter. Beat thoroughly. (This makes a very sticky dough.) Turn into a greased 1 lb. loaf tin. Brush top with remaining beaten egg and sprinkle with demerara sugar. Bake at 350 deg. F., Gas No. 4, for 1 hour 5 minutes until golden brown and sounds hollow when tapped underneath.

Serve sliced, spread with butter.

Nut and Honey Teabread
Makes 10 – 12 slices
Oven temperature 325 deg. F., Gas No. 3

12 oz. self-raising flour
½ teaspoon salt
1 teaspoon ground nutmeg
3 oz. caster sugar
2 oz. walnuts, chopped

2 oz. glacé cherries, chopped
2 eggs
2 tablespoons clear honey
¼ pint milk
2 oz. butter, melted

Grease and line a 2 lb. loaf tin. Sift flour, salt and nutmeg into a bowl. Add sugar, walnuts and cherries and make a well in the centre. Blend together eggs, honey, milk and melted butter and stir into flour mixture to make a soft dough. Turn into prepared tin and bake at 325 deg. F., Gas No. 3, for 1¼ hours. Turn out and cool.

Serve sliced, spread with butter.

Spiced Banana Loaf
Makes 10 – 12 slices
Oven temperature 350 deg. F., Gas No. 4

8 oz. self-raising flour
½ teaspoon salt
½ teaspoon mixed spice
2 oz. glacé cherries, washed, dried and quartered
2 oz. shelled walnuts, chopped
1 oz. candied peel, chopped

4 oz. butter
4 oz. soft brown or caster sugar
2 eggs
1 rounded tablespoon clear honey
1 lb. ripe bananas, peeled and mashed
4 oz. sultanas

Grease and line a 2 lb. loaf tin. Sift flour, salt and spice into a bowl. Add cherries, walnuts and peel. In another bowl beat butter and sugar until light and creamy. Beat in eggs a little at a time, then honey. Stir in flour and all other ingredients. Turn into prepared tin and bake at 350 deg. F., Gas No. 4, for 1 hour. Reduce oven temperature to 300 deg. F., Gas No. 2, and bake for a further 30 – 40 minutes or until a skewer inserted in centre comes out clean. Turn cake out and cool on a wire tray. Serve sliced and generously buttered.

Orange Spice Cake

Oven temperature 375 deg. F., Gas No. 5

	Icing
6 oz. self-raising flour	1 small orange
1 teaspoon mixed spice	2 oz. butter
1 orange	12 oz. icing sugar, sieved
6 oz. butter	
6 oz. caster sugar	crystallised orange slices and whole walnuts for decoration
3 eggs, beaten	

Sift together flour and mixed spice. Grate rind and squeeze juice from orange. Beat butter and sugar together until light and creamy. Add grated orange rind and beat in eggs, a little at a time, adding a tablespoon of the flour with the last addition. Fold in flour mixture and finally stir in 4 tablespoons of orange juice. Divide between two greased 8 inch sandwich tins and bake at 375 deg. F., Gas No. 5, for 25 minutes. Cool on a wire tray.

To make icing grate rind and squeeze juice from orange. Melt butter over a low heat until just melted. Add grated orange rind, 2 tablespoons of juice and 6 oz. of the icing sugar and beat until smooth. Gradually beat in remaining icing sugar until mixture reaches a spreading consistency. Use a little of the icing to sandwich the sponges together. Spread remaining icing over top and sides of cake and swirl with a round-ended knife. Decorate with crystallised orange slices and whole walnuts.

Family Fruit Cake

Oven temperature 350 deg. F., Gas No. 4

8 oz. self-raising flour
$\frac{1}{4}$ teaspoon salt
$\frac{1}{2}$ teaspoon mixed spice
6 oz. butter
6 oz. caster sugar
grated rind of 1 orange

3 eggs, blended
12 oz. sultanas
3 tablespoons milk
2 tablespoons orange juice

Grease and line a 7 inch cake tin. Sift flour, salt and spice into a bowl. In another bowl beat butter, sugar and orange rind until light and creamy. Beat in eggs a little at a time. Fold in sifted flour, then sultanas. Add milk and orange juice. Turn mixture into prepared tin and bake at 350 deg. F., Gas No. 4, for 1$\frac{1}{2}$ hours or until a skewer inserted in centre comes out clean. Turn out onto a wire tray to cool. Store in an airtight tin or wrapped in foil until needed.

Glazed Fruit Cake

Oven temperature 325 deg. F., Gas No. 3

5 oz. self-raising flour
3 oz. plain flour
$\frac{1}{2}$ teaspoon salt
$\frac{1}{4}$ teaspoon mixed spice
$\frac{1}{4}$ teaspoon cinnamon
6 oz. butter
6 oz. caster sugar
grated rind of 1 lemon
4 eggs, beaten
10 oz. sultanas
2 oz. stoned dates, chopped

Glaze
1 rounded tablespoon golden syrup
1 tablespoon lemon juice

Decoration
7 glacé pineapple rings
3 oz. glacé cherries, halved

Line an 8 inch round cake tin with greased greaseproof paper. Sift together flours, salt and spices. Beat together butter, sugar and lemon rind until light and creamy. Add egg, a little at a time, beating well after each addition. Fold in sifted ingredients alternately with fruit. Turn mixture into prepared tin, bake at 325 deg. F., Gas No. 3, about 1$\frac{1}{2}$ – 2 hours or until a skewer inserted in centre comes out clean. Leave to cool in tin for 10 minutes then turn out onto wire tray to finish cooling. Store in airtight container until day before required, then prepare glaze. Put ingredients for glaze in pan, bring slowly to boiling point, simmer 2 minutes. Brush top of cake with glaze. Arrange pineapple rings close together in centre of cake, place a half cherry in centre of each ring.

Arrange remaining cherries round edge of cake to cover top completely. Brush glacé fruits liberally with glaze.

Leave to set before serving.

Traditional Christmas Cake

Oven temperature 300 deg. F., Gas No. 2

8 oz. butter

8 oz. soft brown sugar

4 eggs

9 oz. plain flour

$\frac{1}{4}$ teaspoon salt

$1\frac{1}{2}$ tablespoons black treacle

12 oz. currants

12 oz. stoned raisins

8 oz. sultanas

6 oz. glacé cherries, quartered

2 oz. candied peel, chopped

2 oz. almonds, blanched and chopped

1 teaspoon mixed spice

$\frac{1}{4}$ teaspoon ground nutmeg

2 tablespoons brandy

Almond paste

12 oz. ground almonds

6 oz. icing sugar

6 oz. caster sugar

$\frac{1}{4}$ teaspoon almond essence

4 egg yolks

3 teaspoons lemon juice

4 tablespoons apricot jam, warmed and sieved

Royal icing

3 egg whites

1 lb. 8 oz. icing sugar, sieved

1 teaspoon lemon juice

$1\frac{1}{2}$ teaspoons glycerine

Line an 8 inch round tin with two layers of greased greaseproof paper. Tie a band of brown paper round the outside. Cream butter and sugar together until pale. Beat in eggs gradually, adding 1 tablespoon flour to prevent the mixture curdling. Fold in flour, salt, treacle, dried fruit, cherries, peel, nuts and spices. Turn into the prepared tin. Bake at 300 deg. F., Gas No. 2, for 3 hours, then lower oven temperature to 250 deg. F., Gas No. $\frac{1}{2}$, and cook for a further hour or until a skewer inserted in centre of cake comes out clean. Leave to cool in tin for 10 minutes then turn out onto a wire tray. When almost cold turn upside down and spoon brandy over base. Store, wrapped in greaseproof paper and foil, until needed.

Mix all ingredients, except apricot jam, for almond paste in a bowl to form a smooth paste. Divide in two. Roll one half on a sugared board to a circle same size as cake. Roll other half to a strip the depth of cake and long enough to go round sides. Brush cake with sieved apricot jam. Put circle of paste on top and strip firmly round sides. Leave to dry at least 3 days before icing.

Whisk egg whites for royal icing in a bowl until frothy. Gradually beat in icing sugar. Finally beat in lemon juice and glycerine. Place cake on a silver board. Spread icing over top and sides of cake, pulling it into peaks with the handle of a teaspoon. Leave to set overnight. Arrange a decoration on top, if liked.

Hazelnut Layer Cake

Oven temperature 375 deg. F., Gas No. 5

7 oz. self-raising flour

$\frac{1}{4}$ teaspoon salt

$\frac{1}{4}$ teaspoon cinnamon

4 oz. shelled hazelnuts, lightly toasted and finely chopped

3 oz. butter

8 oz. caster sugar

2 eggs, separated

8 tablespoons milk

Frosting and filling

10 oz. caster sugar

4 tablespoons water

$\frac{1}{4}$ teaspoon cream of tartar

pinch of salt

2 egg whites

Decoration

few shelled hazelnuts, lightly toasted

Grease and line two 8 inch straight-sided sandwich tins. Sift flour, salt and cinnamon into a bowl. Add 3 oz. hazelnuts, put remainder on one side for filling. In another bowl beat butter and sugar until light and creamy. Beat in egg yolks. Stir in flour and nuts alternately with milk. Whisk egg whites until they form soft peaks. Fold into mixture. Divide between prepared tins and bake at 375 deg. F., Gas No. 5, for 25 minutes or until centres of sponges spring back when lightly pressed. Turn out to cool on a wire tray. Put sugar, water, cream of tartar, salt and egg whites for frosting in top part of a double boiler. Whisk over boiling water until frosting stands in peaks. Remove bowl from heat and continue whisking frosting until it is thick enough to spread. Take out one third of frosting and mix with remaining chopped hazelnuts. Use to sandwich cakes together. Use remaining frosting to coat top and sides of cake. Decorate with whole hazelnuts.

Devil's Food Cake

Oven temperature 350 deg. F., Gas No. 4

6 oz. plain flour

$\frac{1}{4}$ teaspoon baking powder

1 teaspoon bicarbonate of soda

$\frac{1}{2}$ teaspoon ground allspice

2 oz. cocoa

4 oz. butter

10 oz. caster sugar

2 eggs, beaten

$\frac{1}{2}$ pint, less 4 tablespoons water

Chocolate butter cream

$1\frac{1}{2}$ oz. butter

2 oz. icing sugar, sieved

$1\frac{1}{2}$ oz. plain chocolate

1 teaspoon water

Frosting

1 lb. caster sugar

$\frac{1}{4}$ pint water

2 egg whites

Grease two 8 inch sandwich tins and line with circles of greased greaseproof paper. Sift together flour, baking powder, bicarbonate of soda, allspice and cocoa. Beat butter until light then gradually beat in sugar. Add eggs a little at a time, beating well. Fold in flour alternately with water. Divide cake mixture between tins and bake at 350 deg. F., Gas No. 4, for about 55 – 60 minutes. Turn out and cool on wire tray.

Beat butter well for butter cream, gradually beat in icing sugar. Melt chocolate with water in a basin over hot water. Beat into butter and sugar. Use to sandwich cakes together.

Dissolve sugar in water in a pan over a low heat. Then boil rapidly to 240 deg. F. To test drop a little of the syrup into a cup of cold water, it should form a soft ball and the water remains clear. Whisk egg whites until very stiff then pour on syrup very slowly whisking all the time. Continue whisking until thick and creamy. Stand for 5 minutes with the surface covered with polythene or wet greaseproof paper. Pour over cake to completely cover. Swirl or rough up with a knife.

Leave for 3 – 4 hours to set.

Gingerbread Meringue House

Oven temperature 325 deg. F., Gas No. 3

12 oz. plain flour
1 teaspoon bicarbonate
of soda
2 teaspoons ground ginger
2 oz. sultanas
3 oz. butter
3 oz. syrup

3 oz. black treacle
4 oz. soft brown sugar
1 egg, beaten with 3 yolks
1 – 2 teaspoons milk

Meringue
3 egg whites
3 oz. caster sugar

Sift flour, bicarbonate of soda and ginger. Mix in sultanas. Melt butter in a large saucepan, add syrup, treacle and brown sugar and heat gently until sugar dissolves. Remove from heat and add flour mixture and eggs. Beat thoroughly and add enough milk to make a dropping consistency. Pour into a greased 2 lb. loaf tin and bake at 325 deg. F., Gas No. 3, for about 1 hour 5 minutes. Remove from tin and place on a baking tray. Allow to cool slightly whilst making the meringue. Reduce temperature of oven to 300 deg. F., Gas No. 2.

Whisk egg whites until stiff and dry. Whisk in the sugar, gradually, so that the meringue becomes thick and stands in peaks.

Place some of the meringue into a piping bag fitted with a fine plain writing nozzle. Pipe the outline of doors and windows on the sides of the cake and using a palette knife and the remaining meringue, shape the roof and chimney pot of the house on top of the cake.

Place the completed house in the oven for 15 minutes, until the meringue begins to dry. Place carefully on a board for serving and leave until quite cold.

Ceylon Tea Cup Cakes

Makes about 14

Oven temperature 375 deg. F., Gas No. 5

2 oz. butter, softened
1½ oz. soft brown sugar
1 tablespoon black treacle
1 tablespoon syrup
1 egg
5 oz. plain flour
½ teaspoon bicarbonate of soda
1 teaspoon mixed spice

1 oz. drinking chocolate
3 tablespoons milk

Icing

4 oz. icing sugar, sieved
1 teaspoon lemon juice
2 teaspoons water
glacé cherries

Place all ingredients in a large mixing bowl and beat well for 2 minutes. Half-fill cup cake cases with mixture. Bake at 375 deg. F., Gas No. 5, for 20 – 25 minutes. Cool. Mix together all ingredients for icing, except cherries. Decorate tops of cakes with a teaspoon of icing and place a piece of glacé cherry in the centre.

Gingernut Men

Makes 8

Oven temperature 375 deg. F., Gas No. 5

6 oz. plain flour
¼ teaspoon salt
1 tablespoon ground ginger
1 teaspoon mixed spice
2 oz. butter

4 oz. demerara sugar
3 – 4 tablespoons syrup, warmed
glacé cherries

Sift together flour, salt and spices. In a separate bowl cream butter and sugar. Mix in flour and enough syrup to form a stiff dough. Roll out to ½ inch thickness and cut out the men with a shaped biscuit cutter. Place carefully on a greased baking tray and bake at 375 deg. F., Gas No. 5, for 15 minutes. Remove and allow to cool. Cut very small pieces of glacé cherry and use to represent buttons.

Almond Apple Cakes

Makes 12

Oven temperature 375 deg. F., Gas No. 5

12 oz. cooking apples	4 oz. butter
½ oz. butter	4 oz. sugar
½ oz. soft brown sugar	2 eggs, beaten
½ teaspoon mixed spice	about 2 teaspoons milk
4 oz. self-raising flour	12 whole blanched almonds
½ teaspoon salt	for decoration
2 oz. ground almonds	

Peel, core and slice apples. Melt butter, sugar and mixed spice together in a large saucepan. Add apple slices and cook gently, covered, until apples are soft but not completely broken up.

Sift flour and salt together and add ground almonds. Cream butter and sugar until light and creamy. Gradually add eggs, beating well between each addition. Add 1 tablespoon of the flour mixture with the last addition of egg. Fold in rest of flour and almond mixture. Add enough milk to give dropping consistency. Spoon half the mixture into twelve 2 inch paper cake cases.

Make a well in the centre of each and fill with 2 teaspoons of apple mixture. Cover very carefully with remaining sponge mixture and top each with a whole blanched almond. Bake at 375 deg. F., Gas No. 5, for 25 – 30 minutes until firm to the touch. Remove and cool on a wire tray.

Cinnamon Soufflette

Oven temperature 375 deg. F., Gas No. 5

2 eggs	2 oz. icing sugar
2½ oz. sugar	2 tablespoons pineapple
2 oz. flour	or apricot jam
2 teaspoons cinnamon	icing sugar for topping
2 oz. butter	

Place eggs and sugar in a basin and whisk over a pan of hot water until thick and creamy. Remove and continue whisking until cool. Sift flour and cinnamon twice, then lightly fold into egg mixture. Pour into a greased 7 inch sandwich tin and bake at 375 deg. F., Gas No. 5, for 20 minutes until sponge springs back when a finger is lightly pressed in the centre. Cool on a wire tray.

Beat butter until light and creamy. Continue beating adding sieved icing sugar gradually. Stir in jam.

Split cake and sandwich together with butter cream. Dust top of cake with sieved icing sugar.

Ginger Sticky-topped Cake

Oven temperature 350 deg. F., Gas No. 4

Topping	*Sponge*
2 oz. butter	4 oz. self-raising flour
1 rounded tablespoon syrup	1 teaspoon baking powder
1 oz. soft brown sugar	2 teaspoons ground ginger
1½ oz. flaked almonds	½ teaspoon salt
1½ oz. glacé cherries, halved	4 oz. caster sugar
1 oz. sultanas	2 eggs
	4 oz. margarine, well-softened

Melt butter, syrup and brown sugar in a saucepan. Add almonds, glacé cherries and sultanas. Pour into the bottom of a greased 2 lb. loaf tin.

Sift flour, baking powder, ginger and salt into a bowl. Add caster sugar, eggs and margarine. Beat thoroughly for 2 minutes. Pour into the tin, carefully covering the topping. Bake at 350 deg. F., Gas No. 4, for 45 – 50 minutes until firm to touch. Turn out and cool on a wire tray.

Cinnamon Apricot upside-down-cake

Oven temperature 350 deg. F., Gas No. 4

1 oz. butter	3 – 4 glacé cherries, halved
2 teaspoons cinnamon	4 oz. butter
1 oz. soft brown sugar	4 oz. caster sugar
15 oz. can apricot halves, drained	2 eggs, beaten
	4 oz. self-raising flour

Melt 1 oz. butter, cinnamon and brown sugar in a saucepan. Pour into the base of a greased 7 inch round cake tin. Arrange apricot halves on top with cherry halves between.

Beat butter and caster sugar until light and creamy. Add beaten eggs, a little at a time, beating well with each addition. Add 1 tablespoon of flour with the last addition of egg. Carefully fold in flour. Pour mixture into cake tin. Level off top and bake at 350 deg. F., Gas No. 4, for 45 – 50 minutes. Turn out and cool on a wire tray.

Ginger and Almond Tuiles
Makes 6 – 8
Oven temperature 425 deg. F., Gas No. 7

2 oz. flaked almonds	1 tablespoon plain flour
2 oz. caster sugar	1 teaspoon ground ginger
1 egg white	

Mix all the ingredients together and stir thoroughly for one minute. Put teaspoons of mixture onto a greased baking tray, allowing plenty of room for spreading.

Bake at top of oven at 425 deg. F., Gas No. 7, for 5 – 7 minutes, until tuiles are golden brown. Remove from tray very gently with a palette knife. Place over a rolling pin and leave until crisp. This gives them the traditional tuile shape.

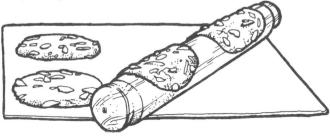

Cinnamon Pineapple Gâteau

Oven temperature 325 deg. F., Gas No. 3

4 oz. self-raising flour	2 eggs
1 teaspoon baking powder	$\frac{1}{4}$ pint double cream
2 teaspoons cinnamon	15 oz. can pineapple
4 oz. caster sugar	tit-bits, drained
4 oz. margarine, well-softened	angelica

Sieve dry ingredients into a large mixing bowl. Add margarine and eggs. Beat for 2 – 3 minutes. Divide mixture equally between 2 greased 7 inch sandwich tins. Bake at 325 deg. F., Gas No. 3, for 25 – 30 minutes until firm to touch. Cool on a wire tray.

Whip cream until stiff. Spread one sponge with half the cream and arrange a layer of half the pineapple pieces on top. Sandwich sponges together and spread remaining cream on the top. Decorate with rest of the pineapple and angelica leaves.

Coffee Cinnamon Feathered Biscuits

Makes 16

Oven temperature 350 deg. F., Gas No. 4

4 oz. plain flour	1 egg, separated
$\frac{1}{2}$ teaspoon cinnamon	6 oz. icing sugar, sieved
4 oz. butter	2 teaspoons coffee essence
3 oz. sugar	1 – 2 teaspoons water

Sift together flour and cinnamon. Beat butter and sugar, until light and creamy. Add egg yolk, flour and cinnamon and knead to a soft dough. Roll out to $\frac{1}{4}$ inch thickness and cut out rounds with a $2\frac{1}{2}$ inch fluted biscuit cutter. Re-roll trimmings and cut out remaining rounds. Place on a greased baking tray and bake at 350 deg. F., Gas No. 4, for 15 minutes. Cool on a wire tray.

To make feathered topping whisk egg white until fluffy, stir in 5 oz. of icing sugar and beat thoroughly. To half of this add coffee essence and remaining 1 oz. of icing sugar. If necessary, add water to give a piping consistency. Place in piping bag fitted with a fine writing pipe.

Spread white icing over tops of biscuits, pipe lines of coffee icing over this at $\frac{1}{2}$ inch intervals. Using a fine skewer draw lines across coffee lines, first one way then the other, to make an attractive feathered appearance. Leave to set.

Spicy Oat Crunchies
Makes 18
Oven temperature 325 deg. F., Gas No. 3

5 oz. butter
2 oz. black treacle
2 teaspoons mixed spice
4 oz. sugar
2 oz. rolled oats
3 oz. desiccated coconut

4 oz. plain flour
2 teaspoons bicarbonate of soda
1 tablespoon hot water
18 whole blanched almonds for decoration

Put butter, treacle, mixed spice and sugar in a pan and warm gently. Remove from heat and stir in oats, coconut and flour. Dissolve bicarbonate of soda in hot water and add to mixture. Leave to cool for a few minutes. Roll into 18 balls and place well apart on greased baking trays. Flatten slightly and place a whole almond in the centre of each. Bake at 325 deg. F., Gas No. 3, for about 25 – 30 minutes until evenly browned. Leave on baking trays for a few moments to set before removing to a wire tray.

Chocolate Allspice Brownies
Makes 15
Oven temperature 375 deg. F., Gas No. 5

4 oz. self-raising flour
$\frac{1}{4}$ teaspoon salt
$\frac{1}{2}$ teaspoon ground allspice
$1\frac{1}{2}$ oz. cocoa
4 oz. butter
8 oz. soft brown sugar
2 eggs, blended
1 tablespoon milk

Chocolate fudge icing
$1\frac{1}{2}$ oz. butter
1 oz. cocoa
3 tablespoons evaporated milk
4 oz. icing sugar, sieved

Grease a 7" × 11" swiss roll tin. Sift together flour, salt, allspice and cocoa. In another bowl beat butter and sugar together until light and creamy. Add eggs, a little at a time, beating well after each addition. Fold in sifted flour mixture with milk, mix well. Turn into prepared tin. Bake at 375 deg. F., Gas No. 5, about 35 minutes or until centre of sponge springs back when lightly pressed. Allow to cool in tin. Melt butter for icing in a pan. Add cocoa. Cook over low heat 1 minute. Remove from heat. Add evaporated milk and icing sugar and mix in thoroughly. Spread over cake in tin and leave to set. When set, cut in 15 squares.

Anise Seed Florentines
Makes 12

Oven temperature 350 deg. F., Gas No. 4

2 oz. syrup
2 oz. caster sugar
2 oz. butter
2 teaspoons anise seed
2 oz. plain flour

$\frac{1}{2}$ oz. chopped mixed peel
$\frac{1}{2}$ oz. glacé cherries, chopped
$\frac{1}{2}$ oz. flaked almonds

Warm syrup, sugar and butter together in a saucepan until sugar dissolves. Remove from heat. Stir in anise seed, flour, mixed peel, cherries and nuts. Spoon teaspoons of mixture onto a well-greased baking tray, well apart to allow for spreading. Bake at 350 deg. F., Gas No. 4, for about 20 minutes until golden brown. Remove from oven and leave on tray for 1 – 2 minutes to set. Lift off carefully with a palette knife and leave to cool on wire tray.

Party Brandy Snaps
Makes 16

Oven temperature 325 deg. F., Gas No. 3

2 oz. butter
2 oz. sugar
2 oz. syrup
1 teaspoon ground ginger

2 oz. plain flour
$\frac{1}{2}$ pint double cream
2 oz. chopped mixed peel

Melt butter, sugar and syrup in a saucepan. Add ginger and flour, mix well. Place teaspoons of mixture, well apart, on a well-greased baking tray and bake at 325 deg. F., Gas No. 3, for 7 – 10 minutes. Remove from oven, leave for about 1 minute then loosen from tray and quickly roll each brandy snap round the greased handle of a wooden spoon. Leave until cold.

Whisk cream until stiff, fold in chopped mixed peel. Spoon into a piping bag fitted with a $\frac{1}{2}$ inch plain nozzle and pipe the cream into the ends of each brandy snap.

Pickles
&
Chutneys

Spiced Vinegar

1 teaspoon cinnamon	10 whole allspice
12 whole cloves	2 pints distilled malt
1 teaspoon ground mace	vinegar

Put spices and vinegar in a pan. Bring slowly to boiling point then remove from heat. Pour into a large china or toughened glass bowl, cover with a plate. Leave to steep at least 2 hours. Strain before use.

Use to pickle onions, eggs, red cabbage.

Pickled Onions

small silver onions or shallots	spiced vinegar (see recipe above)
brine	sugar
crushed chillies	

Peel and cover onions or shallots with brine. Leave 24 hours then drain, rinse and dry thoroughly. Place onions or shallots in jars. Add $\frac{1}{4}$ teaspoon crushed chillies to each jar, cover with spiced vinegar to which 2 oz. granulated sugar per quart has been added. Cover jars with waxed paper. Leave to mature 1 month before using.

To make brine Dissolve 1 lb. salt in 1 gallon hot water. Strain and use when cold.

Pickled Cucumber with Dill
Makes 2 lb.

1 large cucumber, peeled and sliced	1 teaspoon dill seed
1 oz. salt	$\frac{1}{2}$ teaspoon celery salt
4 oz. granulated sugar	6 whole white peppercorns
$\frac{1}{2}$ pint cider vinegar	$\frac{1}{2}$ teaspoon chilli seasoning

Put cucumber slices in layers with salt in a large mixing bowl. Cover and leave several hours or overnight. Drain cucumber thoroughly and dry on kitchen paper. Put sugar in a pan with vinegar and heat gently until sugar has dissolved. Add remaining ingredients with cucumber, simmer for 5 minutes. Pour into clean, hot jars and cover with waxed paper.

Leave to mature 1 – 2 months before using.

Spiced Plums

Makes about 3 lb.

2 lb. cooking plums
rind of $\frac{1}{2}$ lemon, thinly peeled

1 pint spiced vinegar
(see recipe page 137)
8 oz. soft brown sugar

Wash plums and remove stalks. Put in a large enamel pan with lemon rind and spiced vinegar. Cover and slowly bring to simmering point, taking care plums do not boil. Remove plums, draining well, and pack in clean, hot jars. Add sugar to vinegar and boil until syrupy. Pour vinegar into jars, making sure plums are completely covered. Cover with waxed paper. Leave to mature for 2 months before using.

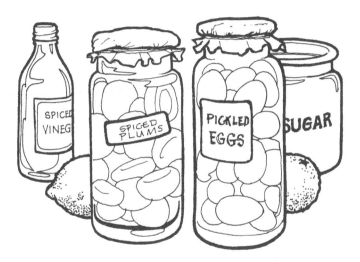

Pickled Eggs

2 pints spiced vinegar
(see recipe page 137)
rind of $\frac{1}{2}$ small orange,
thinly peeled

$\frac{1}{4}$ teaspoon instant minced
garlic (optional)
hard-boiled eggs, cooled
and peeled

Add orange rind and garlic to ingredients when making spiced vinegar.

Pack hard-boiled eggs in wide-necked jars and completely cover with cold spiced vinegar. Cover with waxed paper. Leave to mature 3—4 weeks before using.

Pickled Apples

Makes about 4 lb.

1 lb. soft brown sugar
1 pint distilled malt vinegar
12 whole cloves, tied in
muslin bag

2 teaspoons cinnamon
5 lb. dessert apples,
peeled, quartered and
cored

Put sugar, vinegar and spices into a pan. Bring slowly to boiling point and boil for 15 minutes. Add apples to pan and cook slowly until tender. Remove bag of cloves. Drain apples well and place in hot jars. Boil syrup gently until slightly thick. Strain over apples. Cover jars with waxed paper. Leave to mature 1 month before using.

Chunky Green Tomato Chutney

Makes about 8 lb.

2 lb. green tomatoes,
skinned and chopped
3 pints distilled malt
vinegar
3 lb. cooking apples,
peeled and chopped
2 lb. onions, finely
chopped

1 lb. seedless raisins
1 lb. 6 oz. soft brown sugar
1 tablespoon mustard powder
1 tablespoon salt
1 tablespoon ground ginger
1 teaspoon cayenne

Put tomatoes in a large pan with half of vinegar and simmer until soft. Add remaining ingredients and vinegar. Bring mixture to boiling point, simmer uncovered about 30—40 minutes until fairly thick and pulpy. Pour chutney into clean, hot jars. Cover with waxed paper. Leave to mature 2 months before using.

Red Tomato Chutney

Makes about 5 lb.

8 lb. ripe tomatoes,
skinned and chopped

8 oz. onions, finely
chopped

$\frac{3}{4}$ pint spiced vinegar
(see page 137)

1$\frac{1}{2}$ teaspoons paprika

$\frac{1}{8}$ teaspoon cayenne

1 oz. salt

1 lb. granulated sugar

Put tomatoes in a pan with onions, cover and simmer until thick and pulpy. Add half of vinegar, then spices and salt and simmer until thick. Put sugar in another pan with remaining vinegar, heat gently until sugar has dissolved. Add to tomato mixture, simmer until thick. Pour into clean, hot jars and cover with waxed paper. Leave to mature 1 month before using.

Apricot Chutney

Makes about 3 lb.

1 lb. dried apricots

1 large onion, chopped

1$\frac{1}{4}$ tablespoons salt

$\frac{1}{4}$ teaspoon cayenne

4 oz. demerara sugar

4 oz. sultanas

1 pint distilled malt vinegar

grated rind and juice
of 1 lemon

1 oz. pickling spice

$\frac{1}{2}$ teaspoon coriander seed

Soak apricots in cold water overnight, drain and cut each in half. Put apricots in a pan with all ingredients except pickling spice. Tie pickling spice and coriander seed in a piece of muslin, add to pan, cover and simmer 1 hour. Stir mixture occasionally so it does not stick to pan. Remove lid, simmer chutney for a further 20 minutes, stirring frequently. Remove bag of spices from pan. Pour chutney into clean, hot jars. Cover with waxed paper. Leave to mature 1 month before using.

Piccalilli

Makes about 7 lb.

2 cauliflowers
1 small marrow
1 lb. 8 oz. pickling onions
1 lb. tomatoes
1 oz. salt
4 pints malt vinegar
1 lb. 8 oz. demerara sugar

2 oz. mustard powder
2 tablespoons turmeric
1 tablespoon curry powder
1 tablespoon ground ginger
2 tablespoons cornflour

Prepare vegetables and cut into small pieces. Lay in a dish, sprinkle with salt and leave for 12 hours. Drain well. Bring vinegar and sugar slowly to boiling point in a large pan, add vegetables and cook for 10 – 15 minutes or until vegetables are tender. Blend mustard, turmeric, curry powder, ginger and cornflour with a little cold water. Add to rest of ingredients and cook for a further 5 minutes. Pour into clean, hot jars and cover with waxed paper. Leave to mature 1 month before using.

141

Spiced Blackcurrants

Makes two ½ lb. jars

8 oz. fresh blackcurrants
½ pint distilled malt vinegar
3 oz. soft brown sugar
1 teaspoon whole allspice

2 whole cloves
½ teaspoon cinnamon
½ oz. cornflour
2 tablespoons water

Put blackcurrants in pan with vinegar and sugar. Heat gently until sugar has dissolved. Tie spices in a piece of muslin, add to pan and simmer gently for 10 minutes, uncovered. Blend together cornflour and water. Add a little hot blackcurrant juice. Return cornflour mixture to pan. Bring to boiling point, simmer 2 minutes then remove spices. Pour into small, clean, hot jars and cover with waxed paper. Use within 3 months.

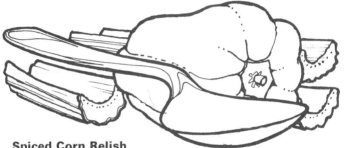

Spiced Corn Relish

Makes about 4 lb.

2 large onions, peeled
4 large sticks celery
1 large green or red pepper, seeded
3 × 12 oz. cans corn kernels
1 lb. granulated sugar
2 teaspoons turmeric
½ teaspoon ground cumin seed

2 teaspoons coriander seed, tied in muslin
½ teaspoon garlic powder
1 tablespoon salt
1 pint distilled malt vinegar

Chop onions, celery and pepper. Put in a large saucepan with all remaining ingredients. Bring to the boil, stirring, until sugar is dissolved. Turn down heat and simmer, uncovered, for 1 hour. Remove coriander seeds. Pour into clean, hot jars. Cover with waxed paper.

Leave to mature 1 month before using.

Country Apple Chutney
Makes about 5 lb.

4 lb. 8 oz. windfall apples, peeled, cored and chopped
2 lb. soft brown sugar
1 lb. 8 oz. onions, chopped
4 pints malt vinegar
1 lb. 8 oz. sultanas or raisins

1 oz. ground ginger
2 teaspoons garlic powder
2 teaspoons mustard powder
1 teaspoon cayenne

Put apples in pan with sugar, onions and vinegar. Bring to boiling point and simmer until pulpy. Add all other ingredients, simmer 10 minutes. Turn chutney into a large bowl, cover and leave in cool place, stirring daily, for 1 week. Put in clean jars and cover with waxed paper. Leave to mature 3 months before using.

Marrow Jam
Makes about 5 lb.

4 lb. marrow, peeled and sliced
3 lb. 8 oz. granulated sugar

2 tablespoons ground ginger

Remove pith from marrow. Cut flesh in small cubes. Put in layers with sugar in a large bowl, cover and leave overnight to draw syrup. Put marrow and syrup in a preserving pan. Bring slowly to boiling point, stirring. Add ginger. Simmer for 50 – 60 minutes until setting point (220 deg. F.) is reached, stirring occasionally. Leave jam to cool for 10 minutes. Pour into clean, hot jars and cover with waxed paper. Use within 6 months.

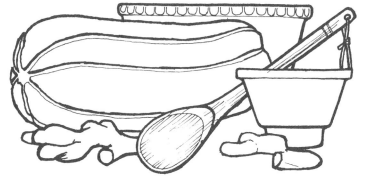

Drinks

Lambswool
Makes 10 – 12 glasses

2 pints brown ale
1 pint medium dry cider
1 teaspoon ground nutmeg

½ teaspoon ground ginger
about 2 oz. soft brown sugar

Mix together all ingredients except the sugar in a large saucepan. Bring to the boil then simmer very gently for 7 – 10 minutes. Sweeten to taste and serve hot.

Spiced Mead
Makes 6 glasses

2 pints cider
2 tablespoons honey
2 tablespoons lemon juice
1 teaspoon ground nutmeg

1 teaspoon cinnamon
1 dessert apple, sliced
1 lemon, sliced

Place all ingredients, except apple and lemon, into a saucepan and bring gently to the boil. Simmer 10 minutes. Strain through muslin and pour into glasses. Add apple slices and halved lemon slices.

Bishop's Cup
Makes 6 glasses

2 lemons
8 whole cloves
2 oz. lump sugar

1 bottle cheap port
¼ teaspoon mixed spice
1 pint boiling water

Stick cloves into 1 lemon. Rub some of the lump sugar over skin of other lemon to extract the zest, then squeeze juice from the lemon. Heat port to nearly boiling point. Remove from heat and add lemon with cloves, sugar, lemon juice, mixed spice and boiling water. Infuse at least 30 minutes. Remove lemon with cloves and re-heat port but do not boil. Remove cloves from lemon, cut lemon into 6 slices. Strain hot port into glasses and place a lemon slice in each glass.

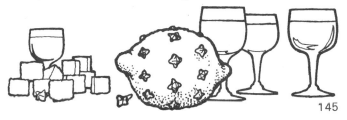

Scottish Punch
Makes 18 glasses

4 oranges
1 bottle whisky
$\frac{1}{2}$ bottle ginger wine
4 oz. clear honey

6 whole cloves
$\frac{1}{2}$ bottle red wine
$1\frac{1}{2}$ pints boiling water

Peel rind thinly from oranges, then squeeze out juice. Put all ingredients, except water, in a large pan. Bring slowly almost to simmering point but do not allow to boil. Strain into a warm punchbowl. Just before serving add the boiling water.

Iced Calypso Coffee
Makes 4 glasses

1 pint fresh black coffee
12 whole allspice
2 cloves

1 small orange
2 – 3 tablespoons caster sugar

Add spices and thinly peeled rind of half the orange to hot coffee and leave to infuse for 1 hour. Squeeze juice from the peeled half of orange and add to coffee. Strain into serving jug. Place two or three ice cubes in 4 tall glasses and pour coffee into glasses. Cut remaining half orange into slices and float on top of glasses.

Mulled Claret
Makes 6 glasses

$\frac{1}{4}$ pint water

4 oz. caster sugar

1 lemon

pinch mint

6 whole cloves

1 bottle claret

2 oranges

few thin slices cucumber

Put water, sugar, thinly peeled lemon rind, mint and cloves into a pan and simmer for 1 hour. Add wine and heat until piping hot, but not boiling. Squeeze juice from oranges and lemon. Strain wine and fruit juices into a jug. Add cucumber and serve at once.

Swiss Gluwein
Makes 6 glasses

2 lemons

1 bottle cheap red wine

1 pint water

8 whole cloves

$\frac{1}{4}$ teaspoon cinnamon

2 – 4 oz. caster sugar

sherry glass of brandy (optional)

Peel rind very thinly from lemons. Cut a few slices of lemon for garnish then squeeze remaining lemons to extract juice. Put lemon rind, juice, wine, water, cloves and cinnamon into a pan, cover and bring to just below simmering point. Leave at this temperature at least 1 hour. Lift out the lemon rind and cloves and add sugar to taste. Add brandy just before serving and serve hot, with lemon slices floating on top.

Chocolate Egg Nog
Makes 1 glass

$\frac{1}{4}$ pint milk

2 teaspoons drinking chocolate

sugar to taste

$\frac{1}{4}$ teaspoon mixed spice

1 egg

Heat milk, drinking chocolate and sugar until hot but not boiling. Whisk together mixed spice and egg in a jug, then whisk in heated milk. Strain into glass.

Negus

Makes 6 glasses

4 oz. soft brown sugar
$\frac{1}{2}$ pint water
12 whole cloves
$\frac{1}{4}$ teaspoon cinnamon
$\frac{1}{4}$ teaspoon ground nutmeg

thinly peeled rind of
1 orange
3 lemons
1 bottle red wine
slices of orange to
decorate

Put sugar and water in a large pan and heat gently until sugar has dissolved. Boil sugar syrup for 5 minutes then add cloves, cinnamon, nutmeg, orange rind and thinly peeled rind of 1 lemon. Simmer for 5 minutes then strain syrup. Squeeze juice from lemons, strain and add to syrup with wine. Heat through then pour into a warm punchbowl. Decorate with orange slices.

Cinnamon Fruit Cup

Makes 6 – 8 glasses

2 oranges
4 lemons
3 oz. caster sugar
$\frac{1}{2}$ teaspoon cinnamon
2 pints boiling water

Decoration
sliced fruit, i.e.
apples, orange, lemon

Start preparing the cup the day before it is needed. Wash and dry fruit. Peel fruit with a potato peeler, taking care to remove none of the pith. Put peeled fruit in a polythene bag in refrigerator. Put peel, sugar and cinnamon in a jug, pour over boiling water. Cover and leave to stand in cold place overnight. Next day cut fruit in half and squeeze out juice. Add juice to peel and water, then strain. Chill well and serve with sliced fruit floating in each glass.

Pomander Ball
or Clove Orange

As a parting thought, here is one way that the delicate aroma of spices can pervade your home.

A pomander ball is often called a clove orange and can be used as a moth-deterrent as well as scenting cupboards and drawers or being used decoratively anywhere in the home. An orange is studded with cloves, rubbed in a mixture of spices, allowed to dry in the dark and is then ready for use or display. The orange does not decay — it just becomes smaller and smaller and hard as iron; it can remain spicily fragrant for years.

You will need: a round, ripe, thin-skinned orange (medium to small); approximately 2 jars of whole cloves; 1 teaspoon ground cinnamon and 1 teaspoon orris powder mixed together; tissue paper, decorative ribbon and $\frac{1}{2}$ inch staples; a sachet of pot-pourri mixture is optional.

Note Orris powder is the powdered dried root of the white flowering Florentine iris, native to the Mediterranean area and

cultivated as well in Persia and north India. It has the sweet scent of violets but a bitter taste.

Pot-pourri is a mixture of dried petals and spices, usually kept in a jar or bowl for perfuming a room.

Orris powder and pot-pourri may be obtained from herbalists.

Stud the orange closely with cloves starting either at the stalk end and working round until it is completely covered, or starting in the middle of the orange and working round in sections. Any broken tops or stalks of the cloves can be ground and used in cooking. When the orange has been completely covered, rub it in the mixture of ground cinnamon and orris powder. Wrap the orange in tissue paper and leave it in a warm, dark place for about a month thus allowing it to dry through completely.

To make your pomander more fragrant, it can then be placed in a little box of pot-pourri mixture and left embedded in it, in a warm, dry place, for a few more weeks.

Shake off any surplus powder (or pot-pourri mixture) and tie a ribbon round the orange ending with a bow or making a loop to suspend it. Alternatively, press a staple into the top of the orange and tie a bow to it, or thread narrow ribbon through the staple and make a loop.

Useful facts and figures

All measurements are B.S.I. Imperial measurements, except where indicated otherwise. All spoon measurements are level.

A plan has been worked out for converting recipes from British measures to their approximate metric equivalents. For ease of measuring it is recommended that solids and liquids should be taken to the nearest number of grammes and millilitres which is divisible by 25. If the nearest unit of 25 gives scant measure the liquid content in a recipe must also be reduced. For example, by looking at the chart below you will see that 1 oz. is 28 g. to the nearest whole figure but it is only 25 g. when rounded off to the nearest number which can be divided by 25.

Ounces	A — Approx. g to the nearest whole figure	B — Approx. to the nearest unit of 25	Ounces	A — Approx. g to the nearest whole figure	B — Approx. to the nearest unit of 25
1	28	25	11	311	300
2	57	50	12	340	350
3	85	75	13	368	375
4	113	125	14	396	400
5	142	150	15	428	425
6	170	175	16	456	450
7	198	200			
8	226	225			
9	255	250			
10	283	275			

Note: When converting quantities over 16 oz. subtract 16 oz. from required quantity, look up difference in column A and add to 456 g (16 oz.), then adjust to nearest unit of 25, using column B as the guide.

Approximate liquid measures

Metric	Imperial
100ml	6 tablespoons (4 fluid ounces)
125ml	8 tablespoons (5 fluid ounces or $\frac{1}{4}$ pint)
150ml	$\frac{1}{4}$ pint plus 2 tablespoons (6 fluid ounces)
200ml	$\frac{1}{2}$ pint less 4 tablespoons (8 fluid ounces)
250ml	$\frac{1}{2}$ pint (10 fluid ounces)
300ml	$\frac{1}{2}$ pint plus 4 tablespoons (12 fluid ounces)
500ml	1 pint less 4 tablespoons (18 fluid ounces)
575ml	1 pint (20 fluid ounces)

Oven temperature chart

	Fahrenheit	Celcius	Gas Mark
Very cool	225	110	$\frac{1}{4}$
	250	130	$\frac{1}{2}$
Cool	275	140	1
	300	150	2
Moderate	325	170	3
	350	180	4
Moderately hot	375	190	5
	400	200	6
Hot	425	220	7
	450	230	8
Very hot	475	240	9

'Centigrade' temperatures are now known as 'Celsius', which it the preferred international term.

Solid measure

British	American
1 lb. butter or other fat	2 cups
1 lb. flour	4 cups
1 lb. granulated or caster sugar	2 cups
1 lb. icing or confectioner's sugar	3 cups
1 lb. brown (moist) sugar	$2\frac{1}{2}$ cups
1 lb. syrup or treacle	1 cup
1 lb. rice	2 cups
1 lb. dried fruit	2 cups
1 lb. chopped meat (firmly packed)	2 cups
1 lb. soft breadcrumbs	4 cups
$\frac{1}{2}$ oz. flour	1 level tablespoon*
1 oz. flour	2 level tablespoons*
1 oz. sugar	1 level tablespoon*
$\frac{1}{2}$ oz. butter	1 level tablespoon*
1 oz. syrup or treacle	1 level tablespoon*
1 oz. jam or jelly	1 level tablespoon

*All U.S. standard measuring tablespoons

British tablespoon and ounce equivalents

Commodity	Tablespoons	Ounces
almonds, ground	3	1
18 almonds whole	–	1
arrowroot	2	1

British tablespoon and ounce equivalents

Commodity	Tablespoons	Ounces
breadcrumbs, dried	6	1
breadcrumbs, fresh	7	1
8 cherries, glacé	–	1
cocoa powder	3	1
coconut, desiccated	4	1
coffee, ground	4	1
coffee, instant	7	1
cornflour	2	1
currants	2	1
curry powder	4	1
custard powder	2	1
flour	3	1
hazelnuts, chopped	3	1
hazelnuts, whole	2	1
honey	1	1
oats, rolled	4	1
peel, cut	1	1
raisins, seedless	2	1
rice	2	1
sugar, caster	2	1
sugar, demerara	2	1
sugar, granulated	2	1
sugar, icing	4	1

British tablespoon and ounce equivalents

Commodity	Tablespoons	Ounces
sugar, soft brown	3	1
sultanas	2	1
syrup	1	1
treacle	1	$\frac{3}{4}$
walnuts, chopped	3	1
8 walnut halves	–	1

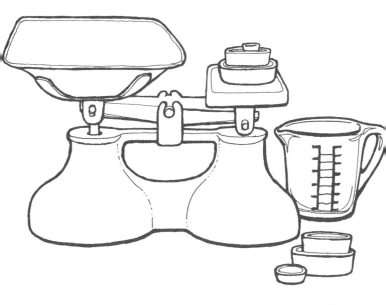

Herbs and Spices index

Recipe index

Creamed celery and ham 94
Glazed sprouts and chestnuts 86
Green peppers Italienne 57
Oven baked chicory with basil 85

Spinach with ham 94
Vegetable casserole 87

Welsh rarebits 101